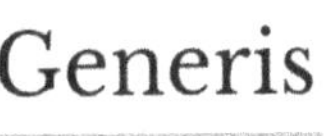

EU JUSTICE AND INTERNAL AFFAIRS AGENCIES

Dragomir Krastev

CIP a Camerei Naţionale a Cărţii

Krastev, Dragomir.

Eu justice and internal affairs agencies / Dragomir Krastev. – Chişinău : Generis Publishing, 2020 (Print on demand). – 143 p.

Referinţe bibliogr.: 138-143.

ISBN 978-9975-153-67-6.

351.74:061.1EU

K 81

Cover image: www.pixabay.com

Generis Publishing
Online orders: www.generis-publishing.com
Orders by email: info@generis-publishing.com

SUMMARY:

INTRODUCTION

The interaction and exchange of information between the national police offices on Schengen territory is much more than the scope of the subordination from the international organization for police cooperation, the co-ordination of the point-by-point contact in the framework of a nationally competent structure on the line for international police cooperation. They come along as a decisive sign on the counteraction tasks to the internationality of the world.

With the development of the international police cooperation that will introduce the new stuff for the interaction, it will provide additional opportunities at the national level to the competent authority for the purpose of public administration and regional security, the guardianship of the societies in the border zones and the counteraction to the accidents with the international element.

Security and the fight against crime has always been a topical issue in European affairs, and mechanisms to develop cooperation between national authorities in this field date back to the late 1970s. Introduced on a purely intergovernmental basis in 1993 as part of the Third Pillar, police and judicial cooperation in criminal matters (PJCCM) has become one of the fastest growing domains of EU action. EU's activities in this field have also entailed an external dimension, through which the European Union (EU) sought to establish and deepen its cooperation with third countries and international organisations.

The EU's activities in criminal matters have been given a new impetus with the entry into force of the Lisbon Treaty. The latter consecrated as one of the objectives of the European Union (EU) ensuring "a high level of security through measures to prevent and combat crime" (Art. 67 (1) TFEU). It also abolished the pillar structure, thus subjecting EU criminal law instruments to the Community method (albeit with few exceptions), and granted the EU new competences to develop its activities in the field of law enforcement and criminal justice. The Lisbon Treaty also singled out the two EU agencies active in the field of PJCCM, Europol and Eurojust. These two agencies, which are working alongside the other EU specialised AFSJ agencies, 2 are the only EU AFSJ agencies whose mandates are defined in EU primary law (Articles 88 and 85 TFEU).

Europol and Eurojust thus deserve further attention. Given their role of supporting and strengthening cooperation between EU Member States in criminal matters, they constitute key participants for EU's internal security and combat against crime. They possess very complementary mandates and competences. Even though this may lead to overlaps and tensions between them, it also imply that their joint participation in a case often gives a value results and increase the chances of a successful outcome. The two agencies are also taking part in the EU's efforts to promote cooperation in criminal matters with external partners, like other agencies, such as Frontex, do in their respective fields of competences. Europol and Eurojust have developed within their respective mandates tools and expertises that are crucial for the success of cross-border investigations and prosecutions, and which make them interesting partners from the perspective of third countries and international organisations. Both agencies have concluded agreements with external partners, forming the basis for diverse forms of cooperation.

The research objective is to assess the legal framework organising the mandate and work of Europol and Eurojust, and more particularly the provisions regulating their external activities in order to determine whether their constitutive instruments are appropriate to meet the challenges ahead. These challenges can be political, as the agencies remain relatively new actors, still in the process of gaining the trust of national (EU and non-EU) authorities, and are not necessarily perceived as potential partners by third countries. Similarly, a third country may prefer not to cooperate with the agencies, and instead to conclude bilateral cooperation agreements with individual Member States – the latter remaining the only ones possessing operational capabilities in the sense of deployable personnel and technical means. These challenges which focuses on the legal challenges encountered by the agencies when they develop their external activities. Even though both Europol and Eurojust are guided by their desire to ensure the efficiency and effectiveness of their cooperation with their external partners, their desire is somewhat constrained by two legal challenges:

They need to accommodate the diversity existing among both EU member States and third countries, while preventing a situation in which differentiation and variable geometry compromise smooth cooperation.

As EU agencies, they are bound by the respect for the rule of the law, the protection of fundamental rights, and data protection rules, enshrined in EU primary law and applicable in the EU's external relations (Art. 20 TEU). They need to strike a delicate balance between the effectiveness of their operational cooperation with external partners and the protection of fundamental rights.

Europol and Eurojust both pre-exist the Lisbon treaty, yet with this new instrument, the two agencies are for the first time mentioned in Articles 85 and 88 TFEU, and their roles and mandates are enshrined in EU primary law. The two agencies can be described as sister agencies involved in the fight against serious cross-border crime affecting two or more EU Member States.

1. European Police Office /EUROPOL/

Europol's mission is to "support and strengthen action by the Member States' police authorities and other law enforcement services and their mutual cooperation in preventing and combating serious crime affecting two or more Member States, terrorism and forms of crime which affect a common interest covered by a Union policy" (Art. 88 (1) TFEU). Europol was set up to gather police and law enforcement information from national authorities and to provide strategic and/or operational analyses on the basis of this information. It has been compared to a 'mega-search engine'. It also coordinates law enforcement authorities' actions, and may support operational activities with its mobile office, analysis in real-time of information gathered on actions days, forensic tools, etc.

Like any EU agency, Europol functions according to a system of controls, checks and balances

Europol is democratically managed on the basis of a system of controls, checks and supervision of governance.

EU justice and interior ministers, MEPs, other EU bodies, a management board drawn from all EU Member States, and its directorate all play important roles in managing Europol and ensuring that it is accountable.

Europol has been an EU agency since 2010. It is ultimately accountable to the Council of Ministers for Justice and Internal Affairs, which comprises the relevant ministers from all EU Member States. The Council is responsible for the main control and guidance of Europol, and appoints the agency's Executive Director and Deputy Directors.

Together with the European Parliament (EP), the Council approves Europol's budget (which is part of the EU's general budget) as well as adopts regulations related to Europol's work.

The EP plays an important role in overseeing Europol. In addition to adopting the agency's annual budget, the EP issues the discharge —

the decision by which it releases the European Commission (EC) from its responsibility for managing a given budget, by indicating the end of the period in which that budget has been executed. The discharge is granted by Parliament on a recommendation from the Council. The EP is also consulted in the adoption of new Council regulations concerning Europol.

Management Board of Europol

An an integral part of Europol's administrative and management structure, the Management Board is the Agency's main governance body and primary stakeholder environment. It provides a unique forum to ensure Europol's continued development as a trusted partner that successfully meets the needs and expectations of the European Union law enforcement community and, in doing so, contributes to a safer Europe.

Its main responsibilities are to provide strategic guidance to the Agency and oversee the implementation of its tasks, to adopt its annual and multi-annual work programmes and annual budget, and to exercise governance responsibilities foreseen in the Europol Regulation.

It is composed of one representative from each EU Member State taking part in the Europol Regulation and one representative from the European Commission (Management Board members). Denmark has an observer status.

The Management Board meets on average four times per year, while its two working groups on corporate matters (WGCM) and on information management (WGIM) meet regularly throughout the year. The Management Board Secretariat provides support to the Chairperson, the Board and its working groups and committees.

In its daily operations, Europol is headed by an Executive Director, who is appointed by a unanimous decision of the Council of Ministers for Justice and Internal Affairs, after the Council has obtained the opinion of the Management Board.

The Executive Director, who is appointed for a four-year term, with the possibility of a second, is responsible for:

- overseeing the administration of Europol
- seeing to the performance of tasks assigned to Europol
- overseeing the management of personnel
- any other tasks consigned to him by the regulation or by the Management Board

FINANCIAL ACCOUNTABILITY

Europol abides by the same principles as other EU agencies and institutions in terms of transparency and financial accountability. A number of institutions and bodies are involved in enforcing financial accountability at the agency, including the:

European Court of Auditors

Internal Audit Service

Internal Audit Capability.

External financial oversight

The monitoring of the commitment and disbursement of expenditures, as well as the establishment and collection of Europol's income, follows the general rules of the EU, such as budgetary discipline and sound financial management.

Europol's annual accounts are subject to an external audit carried out by the European Court of Auditors (ECA). The ECA is an EU institution independent of Europol, as provided for in Articles 285-287 of the Treaty on the Functioning of the European Union (TFEU).

The ECA provides the budgetary authority with a statement of assurance as to the reliability of the accounts and the legality and regularity of the underlying transactions. The ECA draws up an annual report after the close of each financial year. This report, together with the replies from the concerned bodies, including Europol, is published by the ECA in the Official Journal of the EU. It is the basis for the European Parliament, following a recommendation from the Council, to take the above-mentioned discharge decision on Europol's implementation of the budget. The ECA may also at any time to submit observations, particularly in the form of special reports, on specific questions, and to give opinions at the request of another EU institution (referred to in Art. 13 of the TFEU).

Internal oversight

Oversight of Europol is also included in the remit of the Internal Audit Service (IAS), the internal auditor of the European Commission's departments and agencies. As Europol's internal auditor — it doesn't audit the agency for the Commission, but for the agency — the IAS provides a wider, independent view of the accountability procedures within the agency, offering solutions to problems that may arise.

Another level of internal supervision is provided by the Internal Audit Capability (IAC), which operates within Europol and is appointed by and solely accountable to the Management Board. The mission of the IAC is to enhance and protect Europol's organisational value, by providing risk-based and objective assurance, advice and insight. The IAC helps Europol in accomplishing its objectives by bringing a systematic and disciplined approach to evaluate the effectiveness of risk management, control, and governance processes, and by issuing recommendations for their improvement, thereby promoting a culture of efficient and effective management within Europol.

EUROPEAN PARLIAMENT & EUROPEAN COUNCIL

The Joint Parliamentary Scrutiny Group (JPSG) is in charge with the political monitoring and examination of Europol's activity. The JSPG is composed of members of both national parliaments (up to 4 members each) and Members of the European Parliament (up to 16). The Group holds meetings twice a year, prior to which Europol must submit documents related to its actions to be discussed by the JPSG. In these documents, Europol transmits information such as threat assessments, strategic analyses, multiannual programming and annual work programme of Europol and the Consolidated Europol Consolidated Annual Activity Reports (CAAR). The JPSG carries out its activities pursuant to Article 88 of the TFEU.

As part of the JHA, Europol is subject to oversight from Standing Committee on Operational Cooperation on Internal Security (COSI), which ensures that operational cooperation and internal security is promoted and strengthened in the European Union. The role of COSI is to identify possible shortcomings or failures and to adopt concrete recommendations to address them.

EUROPEAN DATA PROTECTION SUPERVISOR

The European Data Protection Supervisor (EDPS) provides assurance that the rights of the individual are protected by the storage, processing and use of data held by Europol. The Europol Regulation reinforces Europol's capabilities. It strengthens procedural safeguards and data protection rights and brings them in line with the changes outlined in the Treaty, ensuring, in particular, that each individual has the right to submit complaints to an independent data protection authority, whose decisions are subject to judicial review.

EUROPEAN OMBUDSMAN

The European Ombudsman provides a further layer of accountability at Europol. The Ombudsman's mission is to serve democracy by working with EU institutions, including Europol, to create a more effective, accountable, transparent and ethical administration. It investigates complaints against EU institutions and bodies.

Any member of the public that has concerns about maladministration in the activities of these institutions and bodies has the right to register a complaint on the matter with the Ombudsman.

EUROPEAN CYBERCRIME CENTRE - EC3

Combating crime in a digital age

Europol set up the European Cybercrime Centre (EC3) in 2013 to strengthen the law enforcement response to cybercrime in the EU and thus to help protect European citizens, businesses and governments from online crime. Since its establishment, EC3 has made a significant contribution to the fight against cybercrime: it has been involved in tens of high-profile operations and hundreds on-the-spot operational-support deployments resulting in hundreds of arrests, and has analysed hundreds of thousands of files, the vast majority of which have proven to be malicious.

While it is difficult to provide reliable estimates, some industry reports suggest that the global cybercrime costs are in the hundreds of billions of euros per year.

Each year, EC3 publishes the Internet Organised Crime Threat Assessment (IOCTA), its leading strategic report on key findings and emerging threats and developments in cybercrime. The IOCTA demonstrates how wide and varied cybercrime is and how EC3 is a key part of Europol's, and the EU's, response. EC3 takes a three-pronged approach to the fight against cybercrime: forensics, strategy and operations.

The EC3 Programme Board provides the Centre with direction as to how to achieve its goals and fulfil its officially assigned tasks, building on partnerships, shared responsibility and cooperation with all Board members.

The Programme Board is the main platform where the activities of the various participants in the domain of strengthening cyber security and fighting cybercrime can be aligned.

Since 2013, within the framework of the European Multidisciplinary Platform Against Criminal Threats (EMPACT) and the EU crime priority "Cybercrime", the leaders of each of the sub-priorities (Cyber Attacks, Child Sexual Exploitation and Payment Card Fraud) have become members as well.

EUROPEAN MIGRANT SMUGGLING CENTRE - EMSC

Managing with the organised criminal groups profiting from migrant smuggling

The EMSC was established in early 2016 following a period of highly dynamic irregular migration, with vulnerable migrants travelling largely unrestricted in significant groups across the Mediterranean Sea, external land borders and further on, into Europe towards their desired destination countries.

Europol specified that many migrants had their journey facilitated by a criminal organisation, at least for the initial sea-journey into Europe. These facilitation services often took the shape of a risky sea crossing in a completely unsuitable and overcrowded vessel. Migrant smuggling quickly evolved into a very lucrative form of criminal enterprise, which circumvents and abuses sea border countermeasures deployed in solidarity by EU Member States and Agencies.

Managing this multi-billion-euro trade thus became an essential part of the EU's response to the migrant crisis. Indeed, the EU's Agenda on Migration (2015) identifies the fight against migrant smuggling is a key priority.

Supporting police and border authorities to coordinate highly complex cross-border anti-smuggling operations therefore became the primary objective of the EMSC, which brought together some of the best investigators in Europe. The EMSC closely cooperates with its partner EU Agencies dealing with judicial cooperation(Eurojust) and border management (Frontex).

EUROPEAN COUNTER TERRORISM CENTRE - ECTC

The hub of expertise is working to provide an effective response to terrorism

Europe is currently facing a vicious, new form of international terrorism. The clear shift in Islamic State's strategy of carrying out special forces-style attacks in the international environment, with a particular focus on Europe, as well as the growing number of foreign terrorist fighters, demonstrates the new challenges facing the EU and its Member States.

To ensure an effective response to these challenges, in January 2016 Europol created the European Counter Terrorism Centre (ECTC), an operations centre and hub of expertise that reflects the growing need for the EU to strengthen its response to terror.

Designed as a hub in the EU in the fight against terrorism, the ECTC focuses on:

- providing operational support upon a request from a EU Member State for investigations;
- tackling foreign fighters;
- sharing intelligence and expertise on terrorism financing (through the Terrorist Finance Tracking Programme and the Financial Intelligence Unit);
- online terrorist propaganda and extremism (through the EU Internet Referral Unit);
- illegal arms trafficking;
- international cooperation among counter terrorism authorities.

INTELLECTUAL PROPERTY CRIME COORDINATED COALITION - IPC3

Stemming the tide of intellectual property crime within and outside the EU

Counterfeit goods are a significant problem that hits the EU particularly hard, accounting for about 5 % of imports. Organised criminal groups are often behind intellectual property crime and thus benefit financially from it.

Fighting intellectual property crime is a key to sustaining jobs and growth in the European economy, and to safeguarding consumers against dangerous and substandard products.

The IPC3, located at Europol and funded by the European Union Intellectual Property Office (EUIPO), is central to the EU's response to this crime area.

The IPC3 provides operational and technical support to law-enforcement agencies and other partners in the EU and beyond, by:

- facilitating and coordinating cross-border investigations;
- monitoring and reporting online crime trends and emerging modi operandi;
- raising public awareness of this crime;
- providing training to law enforcement in how to combat it.

The IPC3 soon produced significant results. At the end of its first year of operation, it was supporting more than 50 high-priority cases of intellectual property infringement. Europol has used it to help take down websites used to sell counterfeit merchandis, to target pirated TV decoders, and to shut down illegal operations using the bitcoin digital currency.

FINANCIAL INTELLIGENCE UNITS – FIU.NET

Coordinated crimes need a coordinated response

FIU.net is a decentralised and sophisticated computer network supporting the Financial Intelligence Units (FIUs) in the European Union in their fight against money laundering and the financing of terrorism.

The need for FIUs is clear: the European single market has fostered free trade, robust competition, a full range of consumer choice, and employment and prosperity. But that has also helped to create the conditions for the free movement of other things and people, such as:

- terrorists
- the proceeds of crime
- funds for terrorism

FIU.net gives Europol and individual FIUs all the tools they need to detect and combat money laundering and the financing of terrorism at the level required to ensure success.

Any country involved in handling cash or value commodities is required to disclose unusual or suspicious transactions to the FIU in its Member State. The FIU analyses the material it receives. If there is a suspicion of money laundering or the financing of terrorism, it forwards the intelligence it has gathered to the national authority responsible for prosecution. As it gathers intelligence, an FIU may have occasion to request information from its counterparts in other Member States. Article 5.4 of the aforementioned Decision stipulates that FIUs "shall undertake. all necessary measures, including security measures, to ensure that information submitted under this Decision is not accessible by any other authorities, agencies or departments" than those it is intended for.

The benefits

FIU.net is designed to facilitate the highly secure connections required for these exchanges of information. Among other things, it allows the individual FIUs to identify connections between the financial intelligence they collect and criminal intelligence stored at Europol. It also brings a host of other benefits, including the following:

• The financing of FIU.net no longer depends on EU Commission grants. Rather, it is integrated into Europol's budget, thus ensuring continuity of operations and allowing for continual improvement of the network.

• Europol can offer its partners both centralised and decentralised options for exchanging information, so information can pass either through Europol or directly from one FIU to another.

• Europol can serve as an information hub within FIU.net.

• Both Europol and individual FIUs can respond rapidly to any situations requiring urgent action.

EU INTERNET REFERRAL UNIT - EU IRU

Monitoring terrorism online

The EU Internet Referral Unit (EU IRU) detects and investigates malicious content on the internet and in social media.

The work of the EU IRU, which is based at Europol's European Counter Terrorism Centre (ECTC), not only produces strategic insights into jihadist terrorism, but also provides information for use in criminal investigations.

Terrorists' use of the internet and social media has increased enormously over the course of recent years. Jihadist groups, in particular, have demonstrated a sophisticated understanding of how social networks operate and have launched well-organised, concerted social media campaigns to recruit followers and to promote or glorify acts of terrorism and violent extremism.

As this is a problem that spans multiple linguistic audiences and jurisdictions, a common EU response was necessary, hence the establishment of the EU IRU in 2015.

The EU IRU has the following core tasks:

• Supporting the competent EU authorities by providing strategic and operational analysis;

• Flagging terrorist and violent extremist online content and sharing it with relevant partners;

• Detecting and requesting removal of internet content used by smuggling networks to attract migrants and refugees;

• Swiftly carrying out and supporting the referral process, in close cooperation with the industry.

The EU IRU comprises of a team of experts with multiple and diverse knowledge and skills, ranging from experts in religiously inspired terrorism, translators, information and communications technology developers and law enforcement experts in counter terrorism.

Since it was set up, the EU IRU has assessed in total 42 066 pieces of content, which triggered 40 714 decisions for referral across over 80 platforms in more than 10 languages*. On average, the content flagged for referrals has been removed in 86% of the cases (* figures of December 2017).

2. European Union Agency for Criminal Justice Cooperation /EUROJUST/

In order to reinforce the fight against serious organised crime, the Tampere European Council of 15 and 16 October 1999, in particular in point 46 of its conclusions, decided on the setting up of a unit that will become Eurojust composed of prosecutors, magistrates or police officers of equivalent competence. As established in Article 3 of the Council Decision of 28 February 2002 setting up Eurojust with a view to reinforcing the fight against serious crime, it has among its objectives:

1. In the context of investigations and prosecutions, concerning two or more Member States, of criminal behaviour referred to in Article 4 in relation to serious crime, particularly when it is organised, the objectives of Eurojust shall be:

(a) to stimulate and improve the coordination, between the competent authorities of the Member States, of investigations and prosecutions in the Member States, taking into account any request emanating from a competent authority of a Member State and any information provided by any body competent by virtue of provisions adopted within the framework of the Treaties;

(b) to improve cooperation between the competent authorities of the Member States, in particular by facilitating the execution of international mutual legal assistance and the implementation of extradition requests;

(c) to support otherwise the competent authorities of the Member States in order to render their investigations and prosecutions more effective.

Regarding organised environmental crime, EUROJUST has adopted some important initiatives in 2013. In November 2013, Eurojust and the European Network of Prosecutors for the Environment (ENPE) co-hosted a meeting entitled "Towards an enhanced coordination of environmental crime prosecutions across the EU: The role of Eurojust in The Hague". Its purpose was to find answers to the question of how to improve best practices and fight organised crime groups involved in environmental crime more effectively. Despite the fact that environmental crime is on the increase, it is not reflected in the level of prosecutions. One of the issues that was explored is the link between environmental crime and organised crime.

In April 2013, the College of Eurojust approved a strategic project on environmental crime that was finished in November 2014. The goals of the project are:

- to assess the status of judicial cooperation;
- to assess the needs of practitioners;
- to identify obstacles and best practice;
- to suggest improvements in the use of existing legal instruments with special focus on penalties, illegal cross-border shipment of waste and trafficking in endangered species;
- to intensify efforts to prosecute environmental crimes at national level;
- and to raise awareness of the added value of Eurojust.

In November 2014, Eurojust adopted the final result of this project, the Strategic Project on Environmental Crime Report that defines environmental crime as "a serious crime, often committed by organised crime groups that affects society as a whole, as its impact is felt not only in the health of humans and animals but also in the quality of air, soil and water". Among other activities, the project drew up and passed a questionnaire to Member States that has also targeted organised crime. The main issues that have been examined in the report are: illegal trafficking in endangered species, illegal trafficking in waste and surface water pollution. The aspects that have been analysed in these three areas are:

- The complexity of legislation relating to protection of endangered species ,
- The level of seriousness and penalties associated with trafficking in endangered species,
- Insufficient coordination among competent authorities at national and international level.

- Burden of proof and evidence gathering.

- Links to organised crime.

The Report has presented as "possible solutions" that should be promoted by Eurojust:

1. Closer international cooperation and involvement of Eurojust.

2. Joint investigation teams and other cooperation tools.

3. Exchange of case law and best practice.

4. Multidisciplinary approach to fighting environmental crime.

5. Harmonisation of definitions standardisation of their interpretation and implementation of dissuasive penalties.

6. Confiscation of criminal proceeds.

7. Cooperation with partners.

Of these possible solutions, the administrative approach as part of the broader multidisciplinary approach is now analysed.

Eurojust's mission is to "support and strengthen coordination and cooperation between national investigating and prosecuting authorities in relation to serious crime affecting two or more Member States or requiring a prosecution on common bases" (Art. 85 (1) TFEU). Eurojust is a 'facilitator' of judicial cooperation, which intervenes to smoothen the effective functioning of judicial cooperation instruments (such as the European Arrest Warrant), to resolve legal issues arising in complex cases (such as conflicts of jurisdiction) and/or to stimulate the coordination of judicial authorities. It has been compared to a 'control tower', whose members will intervene when they notice the need to investigate in a coordinated manner cross-border and/or complex cases. It is important to stress that none of these agencies possesses operational powers. Europol has no vocation of being a European FBI its members have never been enabled to perform investigative acts on the ground. Similarly, Eurojust has no vocation of becoming a European prosecutor, and cannot directly perform investigative or prosecution acts. Nevertheless, they play a key role in assisting national authorities, especially for the coordination of investigations and prosecutions of the multilateral dimension of criminal cases.

The evolution of the two agencies' legal frameworks follows parallel paths, as the Commission proposed back in 2013 two proposals for Regulations. Whereas the Regulation for Europol has been adopted in May 2016 and entered into force on May 1st 2017, the negotiations on the Regulation for Eurojust are not yet finalised. A general approach had been adopted by the Council in February 2015, and the negotiations had been put on hold, pending progresses in the negotiations of the regulation establishing the European Public Prosecutor's Office. The analysis of the future legal framework of Eurojust will thus be based on the text of the General Approach. However, given the recent adoption of the Regulation establishing the European Public Prosecutor's Office, the negotiations on the Eurojust regulation could reach their end soon These new legal instruments pursue several objectives. They not only „lisbonise" the functioning of the agencies, i.e. adapt it to the post-Lisbon Treaty legal framework, but they also give them new tools and competences to further support cross-border cooperation in criminal matters. Such evolution is to be welcomed especially considering the globalization of crime, and the frequency and scale of cross-border criminal activities. Indeed, if the globalization of our economies and societies has created economic growth and wellbeing, it has also given rise to massive opportunities for criminal enterprise and leads to the globalization of crime. Criminals, working either in groups or in networks, operate across continents. Those involved in traditional cross-border criminal activities, such as trafficking in drugs or arms, may produce the illicit substances or weapons in one continent, traffic them across another and market them in a third. Yet, these patterns are also now present in "modern" criminal activities, such as cybercrime, a field in which criminals commit crime anonymously over the Internet, anywhere and anytime, regardless of physical location.

Criminal activities are thus very often limited neither to a single member State nor to the territory of the EU. Terrorism, cyber-crime, migrant smuggling or trafficking in human beings are often mentioned among the most severe transnational criminal threats, especially since they lead to serious violations to their victims' fundamental rights.

These changes in the criminal landscape constitute new challenges for national law enforcement and judicial authorities. They increasingly have to investigate and prosecute cases with cross-border elements and links with neighbouring countries and/or more geographically distant countries. An effective cooperation in criminal matters is thus essential to ensure effective prosecution and conviction of criminals (and thus to ensure the dissuasive effect of criminal law), and to protect the fundamental rights of victims of crime. This necessity in turn impacts the EU and the EU criminal justice agencies Europol and Eurojust. Taking into account the above mentioned evolutions of the criminal landscape, the EU developed the external dimension of its Area of Freedom, Security and Justice, which mainly aims at serving the internal EU security policy by creating a secure external environment in order to combat illegal immigration, terrorism and organised crime. This has led to the emergence of a whole set of instruments, provisions and mechanisms aimed at favouring cross-border cooperation in criminal matters between the European Union, the national authorities of its Member States and its external partners (third countries as well as international organisations). Europol and Eurojust, as EU agencies, participated in this development of the external dimension of the AFSJ. The agencies have benefited from the possibility to develop their cooperation with external partners, notably on the basis of EU secondary law. Their external activities take different forms: the signature of cooperation agreements, allowing or denying the exchange of personal data, the appointment of liaison officers or contact points, or the appointment of liaison magistrates. In practice, even though they remain service providers to the national authorities, and are not automatically involved in all cross-border operations, the two agencies regularly publish press releases detailing the support they offered in cases investigated and prosecuted in cooperation with non-EU Members States. The two agencies are often perceived as the EU structures which come closest to an EU operational capability, which adds to their attractiveness as interlocutor for third countries.

Europol and Eurojust have thus become key players in the development and deepening of cross-border cooperation in criminal matters, not only between national authorities operating in EU Member States, but also between these authorities and those operating in third countries. Their importance has been acknowledged by the EU institutions and the Member States, which have - during the negotiations of the two Regulations - substantially amended the provisions on the agencies' cooperation with third countries and international organisations. These amendments have not only placed the agencies under the general legal framework applicable to the EU's external relations, but they have also introduced new provisions, such as those allowing the exchange of information under derogation clauses. They testify the importance given to the security and the effectiveness of international cooperation in criminal matters in a context where crime prevention sometimes requires real-time transfer of information. These changes are all the more relevant considering that the UK, a key Member State in the field of security, will soon become a third country to the EU, and will rely on the legal framework governing Europol's and Eurojust's external cooperation to continue to cooperate with them.

CONCLUSION

In the current security context, the cooperation with third countries and international organisations is of crucial importance for the EU's objectives of preventing and combating crime. The issue will also be an important point of discussion during the Brexit negotiations, as once the United Kingdom will have withdrawn from the EU, new modalities of cooperation between British authorities and EU agencies will have to be identified. The current modalities of cooperation between Europol, Eurojust and their external partners, which have been analysed in this paper, may serve as a source of inspiration for the EU and UK negotiators. They also reveal the potential limits that may be faced in developing the future modalities of cooperation between the EU and the UK, and the need to reflect on developing specific modalities eventually drawing on the UK's status of former Member State. These issues are of crucial importance, since insufficient cooperation in criminal matters between the EU and the UK may reduce the safety of the people of the UK and of EU citizens.

The two agencies face challenges, starting with the need to accommodate diversity within and outside the European Union. However, their main challenge probably lies in the sensitivity of the exchange of data with third countries that are not bound by the EU norms on the protection of fundamental rights and data protection, and thus potentially entailing severe violations of fundamental rights. The two agencies are not the only actors faced with this challenge, which promises to test the effectiveness of crime prevention against legal considerations, prohibiting the processing of information when it has been obtained in violation of fundamental rights. In today's security reality, marked by regular terrorist attacks, some advocate for looser human rights standards, considering for instance that information preventing an attack shall be used, even though it may have been obtained through torture. In a European Union founded on the respect of the rule of law, such arguments are difficult to uphold. One can welcome in this regard the references in Europol's and Eurojust's regulations to the respect for data protection as a pre-requisite for the reception of personal data from third countries and the transfer of personal data to third countries. In addition, the mechanisms set up to hold both agencies accountable before democratically elected bodies and before judges shall be essential in this regard, in order to ensure that no red lines are crossed. As the Europol Regulation entered into force just a few months ago, and the Eurojust regulation is still under negotiations, it is still too early to provide a definitive answer on whether they are effective and sufficient, and a close attention will need to be paid to their practical implementation.

3. European anti-fraud office /OLAF/

The EUROPEAN ANTI-FRAUD OFFICE was originally set up as a Division of the European Commission for the Resistance to Fraud / UCLAF /. The focus is on the department and the implementation of the investigation in the framework of the financial law enforcement control. President of 1999 UCLAF was reorganized into the European body / agency / for the fight against fraud / OLAF /. The function of the organization will be attributed to those involved in administrative investigations according to the fraud, corruption and all kinds of other illegal activities that are harmful to the financial interests of the Union.

The expansion to the European Union has greatly aggravated the problem of corruption in the EU, and attention has been paid to the action on the body of the department.

The 2004 European Presidency Commission developed an action plan for fighting with fraud in member countries for the period 2004–2005. This measure was limited by the effectiveness of the OLAF and, in particular, the control over the non-negotiable country and the means. budgetary expenditures for the EU, and moreover, such an exchange of information between OLAF, the institution in the EU and the national structure.

What is the mission of OLAF

The European Union budget finances a wide range of programmes and projects which improve the lives of citizens across the EU and beyond. The improper use of funds provided by the EU budget or the evasion of the taxes, duties and levies, which fund the EU budget directly harms European citizens and prejudices the entire European project.

The European Anti-Fraud Office (OLAF) is the only EU body mandated to detect, investigate and stop fraud with EU funds.

OLAF fulfils its mission by:

• carrying out independent investigations into fraud and corruption involving EU funds, so as to ensure that all EU taxpayers' money reaches projects that can create jobs and growth in Europe;

• contributing to strengthening citizens' trust in the EU Institutions by investigating serious misconduct by EU staff and members of the EU Institutions;

• developing a sound EU anti-fraud policy.

What can OLAF investigate

OLAF can investigate matters relating to fraud, corruption and other offences affecting the EU financial interests concerning:

• all EU expenditure: the main spending categories are Structural Funds, agricultural policy and rural development funds, direct expenditure and external aid;

• some areas of EU revenue, mainly customs duties;

• suspicions of serious misconduct by EU staff and members of the EU institutions.

The lifecycle of an OLAF investigation

OLAF receives information about possible fraud and irregularities from a wide range of sources. In most cases, this information results from controls by those responsible for managing EU funds within the European Institutions or in the Member States.

All allegations received by OLAF undergo an initial assessment to determine whether the allegation falls within the remit of the Office and meets the criteria for opening an investigation.

Investigations can involve interviews and inspections of premises and they are classified under one of the following three categories:

• **Internal investigations:** Internal investigations are administrative investigations within the European Union institutions and bodies for the purpose of detecting fraud, corruption, and any other illegal activity affecting the financial interests of the European Communities; including serious matters relating to the discharge of professional duties.

- **External investigations:** External investigations are administrative investigations outside the European Union institutions and bodies for the purpose of detecting fraud or other irregular conduct by natural or legal persons. Cases are classified as external investigations where OLAF provides the majority of the investigative input.

- **Coordination cases:** OLAF contributes to investigations carried out by national authorities or other Community departments by facilitating the gathering and exchange of information and contacts.

After an investigation is concluded, the Office recommends action to the EU institutions and national governments concerned: this usually includes launching criminal investigations, financial recoveries or other disciplinary measures. It then monitors how these recommendations are implemented.

Investigation support

Operational analysis & risk assessment

In the framework of its investigations OLAF analyses information from all relevant sources with a two-fold aim:
- to identify and substantiate cases of fraud and irregularities;
- to monitor, assess and report weaknesses in legislation, contracts, as well as management and control systems.

Its specialist support unit – with analysts, IT and technical staff, computer forensic examiners and others – provides OLAF's investigators as well as other Commission departments and partner authorities in EU countries with analytical support in OLAF casework.

It produces analysis reports on policy areas such as research, administrative expenditure, external assistance, fisheries, and regional risk assessments. These contain an analysis of OLAF's operational findings and a description of irregularities and frauds detected.

Sharing data and expertise

Drawing on its accumulated knowledge and experience, OLAF helps the authorities responsible for managing EU funds – inside and outside the EU – to understand fraud types, trends, threats and risks, and to protect the EU's financial interests by preventing fraud of all kinds.

OLAF gathers data from its own operations, investigations and many other sources. These include:
- Commission audits
- Court of Auditors reports
- national partner authorities
- open sources, such as the internet, press articles and public registers
- commercial sources.

As well as using this information for its own investigations, OLAF shares it through databases and applications: with other Commission departments through the **Irregularity Management System** and with EU Member States through the **Early Detection and Exclusion System**.

Irregularity reporting: Irregularity Management System (IMS)

EU law requires reporting in areas where the EU provides financial support. EU countries must report cases of irregularities in expenditure to the Commission, including suspected and established fraud.

The IMS enables EU countries and candidate countries to report irregularities related **to expenditure to the Commission**. IMS is managed by OLAF. It contains **details offraud** and **irregularities** in the use of funds managed by the national authorities, such as agricultural, European Structural and Investment Funds.

The IMS is open to all Commission departments on a need-to-know basis and is used for the following purposes:

- analysis and reporting (e.g. the annex to the PIF-Report)
- supporting policy initiatives
- supporting OLAF's case selection process
- preparing for audits
- deciding whether to sign off the accounts for previous operational programmes
- replying to questions from the European Parliament.

Early Detection and Exclusion System (EDES)

EDES is a system established by the Commission to reinforce the protection of the Union's financial interests and to ensure sound financial management for direct and indirect expenditure.

EDES aims to:

- ensure the early detection of risks threatening the EU's financial interests
- exclude an economic operator from receiving EU funds
- impose a financial penalty on economic operators breaking EU rules.

Authorising officers can **exclude** unreliable applicants from EU funding or flag suspicions. They do this based on:

- the findings of **OLAF investigations**
- the audit findings of EU institutions and bodies
- reports on irregularities detected by Member State authorities and organisations (e.g. international organisations) that implement EU spending programmes.

EDES has **2 main parts**:

1. **Early Detection**

This part of EDES contains information on people, companies and organisations that could pose a **fraud threat** to the EU's financial interests.

2.   **Exclusion**

The exclusion branch of EDES contains details of people, companies and organisations who are **banned** from **direct and indirect EU funding**

- are bankrupt
- have been found guilty of fraud, corruption or other serious crimes or of serious professional misconduct
- have seriously breached the terms of a previous EU contract.

EU countries and entrusted entities apply their own rules when deciding what action to take if an entity is recorded as 'excluded' in EDES.

Accessing EDES

All authorising officers in EU institutions, bodies and agencies and their staff can access EDES on a need-to-know basis. Read access to the exclusion branch only is available to Member State authorities and entities that implement EU spending programmes.

Casebooks

OLAF produces casebooks of anonymised cases. These highlight:
- fraud indicators ('red flags')
- techniques used by fraudsters ('modus operandi')
- certain work processes that are potentially vulnerable to fraud which may be used in some Commission departments, EU institutions and bodies.

Areas covered so far include:
- internal investigations (2017)
- external aid (2012)
- structural funds (2011)
- research projects (2010)

Casebooks are made available to interested Commission departments and, if relevant, to other institutions and bodies and Member State authorities.

Recommendations

OLAF issues **recommendations on anti-fraud measures** to Commission departments, EU institutions, bodies, offices and agencies. Its recommendations are made:
- based on analysis,
- after an investigation, or
- in response to draft Commission legislative proposals.

If OLAF detects **systemic problems**, it may alert the Commission's internal auditors.

Areas where OLAF has made recommendations include:
- infringement of public procurement rules
- conflicts of interest in recruitment or in the attribution of funds
- research projects (inflated staffing costs, plagiarism, fraudulent use of company names to obtain grants)
- customs transit procedures
- undervaluation of goods
- reimbursement of removal costs of EU staff.

Crawling from OLAF

- cooperation in accordance with international confusion (sub-management)

- Partnership with the Specialized Service (Europol, Interpol, Eurojust, FBI, etc.)

- cooperation and representation in candidate countries

- Improvement in legislation in the oblast on the right to be assisted by a department from a high qualification of right and congregation

- Citizens of Europe can and will help; yes, the guarantee of the establishment of rights is red. They will provide information for isms or indeterminacy on the telephone line.

follow heed:

- Firstly: the statute on the OLAF is mixed: from one country, the organization has respected the rights to fight with fraud and other financial interest interests in the EU, which is really significant for integration into the world.

- Secondly: OLAF is not equipped with a process of legal capacity, someone who sells and is convinced of internal investigations and investigations, in particular, when taking evidence for extortion, someone is inconsistent with competency.

- Thirdly: the benefits from being created and funded on the OLAF can't be mechanically transferred to other conditions, but whitewash along the slopes you need to say yes, let's say it's permissible to be crawled out when you're formed on the structure, you'll be too much to protect on integration structures, similar to the European Union.

In spite of the fact that OLAF is not based on a member of the EU level in the fight with fraud and vandalism, it is therefore limited to being verified by the administrative investigations and presented to the result of the national organization, someone may decide not to take the next steps from the region to punish right.

4. European Union Agency for Cybersecurity (ENISA)

The European Union Agency for Cybersecurity (ENISA) has been working to make Europe cyber secure since 2004. The Agency is located in Athens, Greece and has a second office in Heraklion, Greece.

ENISA is actively contributing to European cybersecurity policy, supporting Member States and European Union stakeholders to support a response to large-scale cyber incidents that take place across borders in cases where two or more EU Member States have been affected. This work also contributes to the proper functioning of the Digital Single Market.

The Agency works closely together with Member States and private sector to deliver advice and solutions as well as improving their capabilities. This support includes inter alia:

- the pan-European Cybersecurity Exercises,
- the development and evaluation of National Cybersecurity Strategies,
- CSIRTs cooperation and capacity building,
- studies on IoT and smart infrastructures, addressing data protection issues, privacy enhancing technologies and privacy on emerging technologies, eIDs and trust services, identifying the cyber threat landscape, and others.

ENISA also supports the development and implementation of the European Union's policy and law on matters relating to network and information security (NIS) and assists Member States and European Union institutions, bodies and agencies in establishing and implementing vulnerability disclosure policies on a voluntary basis.

Since 2019, following the bringing into force of the Cybersecurity Act (Regulation 2019/881), ENISA has been tasked to prepare the 'European cybersecurity certification schemes' that serve as the basis for certification of products, processes and services that support the delivery of the Digital Single Market.

The European Cybersecurity Act introduces processes that support the cybersecurity certification of ICT products, processes and services. In particular, it establishes EU wide rules and European schemes for cybersecurity certification of such ICT products, processes and services.

ENISA's activities

ENISA's approach is further illustrated below by presenting its activities in different areas:
- Recommendations on cybersecurity and independent advice
- Activities that support policy making and implementation
- 'Hands On' work, where ENISA collaborates directly with operational teams throughout the EU
- Bringing together EU Communities and coordinating the response to large scale cross-border cybersecurity incidents
- Drawing up cybersecurity certification schemes

Mission and Objectives

'Securing Europe's Information Society'

The mission of ENISA is to achieve "a high common level of cybersecurity across the Union, including by actively supporting Member States, Union institutions, bodies, offices and agencies in improving cybersecurity. ENISA shall act as a reference point for advice and expertise on cybersecurity for Union institutions, bodies, offices and agencies as well as for other relevant Union stakeholders.

Strategic Objectives

ENISA's strategic objectives are derived from the ENISA regulation, inputs from the Member States and relevant communities, including private sector.

In cooperation and in support to the Member States and the Union institutions,

ENISA in priority seeks to achieve:

#Expertise Anticipate and support Europe in facing emerging network and information security challenges, by collating, analyzing and making available information and expertise on key NIS issues potentially impacting the EU, taking into account the evolutions of the digital environment.

#Policy Promote network and information security as an EU policy priority, by assisting the European Union institutions and Member States in developing and implementing EU policies and law related to NIS.

#Capacity Support Europe maintaining state-of-the-art network and information security capacities, by assisting the Member States and European Union bodies in reinforcing their NIS capacities.

#Community Foster the emerging European network and information security community, by reinforcing cooperation at EU level among Member States, European Union bodies and relevant NIS stakeholders, including the private sector.

#Enabling Reinforce ENISA's impact, by improving the management of its resources and engaging more efficiently with its stakeholders, including Member States and Union Institutions, as well as at international level.

Structure and Organisation

As provided in the Regulation (EU) 2019/881, the bodies of the Agency comprise:

A **Management Board:** The Management Board is ensuring that the Agency carries out its tasks under conditions which enables it to serve in accordance with the founding Regulation.

An **Executive Board:** The Executive Board is preparing decisions to be adopted by the Management Board.

An **Executive Director:** The Executive Director is responsible for managing the Agency and performs his/her duties independently.

A **National Liaison Officers Network**: The NLOs facilitate the exchange of information between ENISA and the EU Member States.

An **Advisory Group:** The advisory group focuses on issues relevant to stakeholders and brings them to the attention of ENISA.

The Regulation 2019/881 also foresees that ENISA shall assist the Commission in providing the secretariat of the European Cybersecurity Certification Group (ECCG) and ENISA shall provide the secretariat of the Stakeholder Cybersecurity Certification Group (SCCG).

Ad hoc Working Groups: The Executive Director establishes, in consultation with the Permanent Stakeholders' Group, ad hoc Working Groups composed of experts. The ad hoc Working Groups are addressing specific technical and scientific matters.

Management Board

The Management Board is composed of representatives of the Member States and the Commission.

The Management Board is entrusted with the necessary powers to:
- Establish the budget
- Verify its execution
- Adopt the appropriate financial rules
- Establish transparent working procedures for decision making by the Agency
- Approve the Agency's work programme

- Adopt its own rules of procedure and the Agency's internal rules of operation
- Appoint and remove the Executive Director

The Management Board is ensuring that the Agency carries out its tasks under conditions which enables it to serve in accordance with the Cybersecurity Act.

Internal rules of procedure for the Management Board and for the Executive Board of ENISA

Management Board composition:
- Chair: Mr Jean Baptiste Demaison, France (CV)
- Commission Representatives
- Member States Representatives
- EEA-Country Representatives (Observers)

List of ENISA Management Board Representatives and Alternates

(Status: 05 June 2020)

Executive Board

On 17 October 2013, the Management Board decided to establish the Executive Board. The Executive Board is made up of five members of the MB and it is chaired by the MB Chairperson.

The Executive Board is preparing decisions to be adopted by the Management Board on administrative and budgetary matters and it meets once every three months.

Advisory Group (AG)

The Advisory Group(AG) is established by Regulation (EU) 2019/881 (Recital 61 and Article 21) of the European Parliament and of the Council of 17 April 2019 on ENISA (the European Union Agency for Cybersecurity) and on information and communications technology cybersecurity certification and repealing Regulation (EU) No 526/2013 (Cybersecurity Act).

Composition

The Advisory Group is composed of "nominated members" and members appointed "ad personam", all in total 33 members from all over Europe. The Management Board, acting on a proposal by the Executive Director, sets up the Advisory Group for a term of office of 2,5 years.

The Role

The ENISA Advisory Group, should focus on issues relevant to stakeholders and should bring them to the attention of ENISA. The ENISA Advisory Group should be consulted in particular with regard to ENISA's draft annual work programme. The composition of the ENISA Advisory Group and the tasks assigned to it should ensure sufficient representation of stakeholders in the work of ENISA.

NLO Network

Set up in 2004 as an informal point of reference into the Member States. As of 27 June 2019 the National Liaison Officers network has become a statutory body of ENISA.

The National Liaison Officers Network facilitates the exchange of information between ENISA and the Member States, and supports ENISA in disseminating its activities, findings and recommendations to the relevant stakeholders across the Union.

The Network is composed of representatives of all member states and will be set up by the Management Board in the course of 2019. ENISA is in the process of implementing a new regulatory framework.

ENISA Transparency Policy

In relation to the External Meeting Calendars of ENISA Management

In the exercise of the ENISA mandate, ENISA managers engage with external public and private stakeholders of the Agency. Key stakeholders include *inter alia* the Member States, the EU Institutions and industry.

In accordance with the legislative framework that is in place, ENISA endeavours to conduct its work as openly as possible and to ensure that it carries out its activities with a high level of transparency.

In the interest of transparency, relevant external meeting calendars of the members of ENISA's management team are made available to the public on the ENISA website

Policies and Procedures

ENISA is committed to operating as an open and transparent organisation. To help citizens and other stakeholders understand how the Agency is managed and held accountable, ENISA publishes a range of documents and other relevant information on its web site.

The Agency realises its commitment to transparency with the publication of documents on ENISA's procedures, its Declaration of Interests, its commitment to the Code of good administrative behaviour, including its annual Work Programme and the Minutes of its Management Board meetings. The publication of procedures allows ENISA to present its working practices and provides the public with insight into the Agency's internal functioning and work environment.

Information regarding procurements and the awarding of contracts is also available on the web site.

Tasks

Frontex, the European Border and Coast Guard Agency, promotes, coordinates and develops European border management in line with the EU fundamental rights charter and the concept of Integrated Border Management.

To help identify migratory patterns as well as trends in cross-border criminal activities, Frontex analyses data related to the situation at and beyond EU's external borders. It monitors the situation at the borders and helps border authorities to share information with Member States. The agency also carries out vulnerability assessments to evaluate the capacity and readiness of each Member State to face challenges at its external borders, including migratory pressure.

Frontex coordinates and organises joint operations and rapid border interventions to assist Member States at the external borders, including in humanitarian emergencies and rescue at sea. The agency deploys European Border and Coast Guard teams, including a pool of at least 1 500 border guards and other relevant staff to be deployed in rapid interventions. The members of the rapid reaction pool must be provided by Member States upon request by the agency. It also deploys vessels, aircraft, vehicles and other technical equipment provided by Member States in its operations. In addition, Frontex may carry out operations on the territory of non-EU countries neighbouring at least one Member State, in case of migratory pressure at a non-EU country's border.

Frontex, the European Border and Coast Guard, supports Member States with screening, debriefing, identification and fingerprinting of migrants. Officers deployed by the agency refer and provide initial information to people who need, or wish to apply for, international protection, cooperating with the European Asylum Support Office

(EASO) and national authorities. It is the national authorities, not Frontex, who decide which person is entitled to international protection.

The agency assists EU Member States in forced returns of people who have exhausted all legal avenues to legitimise their stay within the EU. This help includes obtaining travel documents for the returnees by working closely with consular authorities of the relevant non-EU countries. It can also organise voluntary departures of nationals of non-EU countries who were issued return decisions by Member State authorities. Frontex also organises return operations on its own initiative and "collecting return operations", where returnees are returned with escort officers and transportation provided by their countries of origin. It has created several pools of return experts to be deployed in Member States when needed.

Frontex supports the cooperation between law enforcement authorities, EU agencies and customs at sea borders. Vessels and aircraft deployed in its operations also collect and share information relevant to fisheries control, detection of pollution and compliance with maritime regulations. The agency works closely with European Fisheries Control Agency (EFCA) and European Maritime Safety Agency (EMSA) to implement multipurpose operations. In these operations, vessels and aircraft deployed for border surveillance can also be used for fishing and environmental monitoring.

Frontex focuses on preventing smuggling, human trafficking and terrorism as well as many other cross-border crimes. It shares any relevant intelligence gathered during its operations with relevant national authorities and Europol.

The agency is the centre of expertise in the area of border control. It develops training curricula and specialised courses in a variety of areas to guarantee the highest levels of professional knowledge among border guards across Europe. It also supports search and rescue operations that arise during border surveillance operations at sea.

The ideas that led to the creation of Frontex have a deep history in the European project. Fostering the free movement of people has been an important objective of European integration. In 1957, free movement of goods, persons, services and capital were identified as foundations of the Community in the Treaty of Rome.

During the 1980s, five Member States (Belgium, France, Germany, Luxembourg and the Netherlands) decided to create a common area of free movement – a territory without internal borders. In 1985, they signed the first agreement in a small town in Luxembourg called Schengen – an agreement that was followed in1990 by a Convention implementing the Schengen Agreement.

When the "Schengen area" – a territory in which the free movement of persons - entered into force in 1995, checks at the internal borders were abolished and a single external border was created. Slowly, border control, as well as the rules governing visas and the right to asylum, became common for all Schengen countries.

In order to keep a balance between freedom and security, participating Member States agreed to introduce additional measures focusing on cooperation and coordination of the work of the police and judicial authorities. Because organised crime networks do not respect borders, this cooperation became key to safeguarding internal security.

In 1999, with the signing of the Treaty of Amsterdam, this intergovernmental cooperation was incorporated into the EU framework.

Since 1999 the European Council on Justice and Home Affairs has taken several steps towards further strengthening cooperation in the area of migration, asylum and security.

In the border management field, this led to the creation of the External Border Practitioners Common Unit - a group composed of members of the Strategic Committee on Immigration, Frontiers and Asylum (SCIFA) and heads of national border control services.

The Common Unit coordinated national projects of Ad-Hoc Centres on Border Control. Their task was to oversee EU-wide pilot projects and to implement common operations related to border management.

Two years after the establishment of "ad-hoc" centres the European Council decided to go a step further. With the objective of improving procedures and working methods of the Common

Unit, Council Regulation (EC) 2007/2004 of 26 October 2004 led to the establishment of the European Agency for the Management of Operational Cooperation at the External Borders of the Member States of the European Union (Frontex).

This Regulation was repealed by Regulation (EU) 2016/1624 of 14 September 2016, establishing Frontex, the European Border and Coast Guard Agency.

Regulation (EU) 2019/1896 of 13 November 2019 on the European Border and Coast Guard (OJ L 295, 14.11.2019, p. 1) in turn repealed Regulations (EU) No 1052/2013 and (EU) 2016/1624.

Monitoring & Risk Analysis

Risk analysis is the starting point for all Frontex activities, from high level strategic decision-making to planning and implementation of operational activities.

Frontex collects a wide range of data from Member States, EU bodies, its partner countries and organisations, as well as from open sources on the situation at and beyond Europe's borders. The data is analysed with the aim of creating a picture of the situation at the EU's external borders and the key factors influencing and driving it.

Beyond establishing trends and identifying risks, Frontex also provides advice on appropriate operational responses to various challenges, including cross-border crime, at the EU external borders. This helps optimise the use of available resources and maximise the effcctiveness of actions taken. The agency's risk analysis is used to advise high level decision-making as well for daily coordination of joint operations.

Frontex's risk analysis activities fall into three categories: Strategic Analysis, Operational Analysisand Analytics. Strategic Analysis is aimed mostly at high-level strategic decision-makers, while Operational Analysis supports Frontex-coordinated Joint Operations. The focus of Analytics is the management of collected data and supporting analysts with data and analytical services.

Monitoring & Risk Analysis

Risk analysis is the starting point for all Frontex activities, from high level strategic decision-making to planning and implementation of operational activities.

Frontex collects a wide range of data from Member States, EU bodies, its partner countries and organisations, as well as from open sources on the situation at and beyond Europe's borders. The data is analysed with the aim of creating a picture of the situation at the EU's external borders and the key factors influencing and driving it.

Beyond establishing trends and identifying risks, Frontex also provides advice on appropriate operational responses to various challenges, including cross-border crime, at the EU external borders. This helps optimise the use of available resources and maximise the effectiveness of actions taken. The agency's risk analysis is used to advise high level decision-making as well for daily coordination of joint operations.

Frontex's risk analysis activities fall into three categories:Strategic Analysis, Operational Analysisand Analytics. Strategic Analysis is aimed mostly at high-level strategic decision-makers, while Operational Analysis supports Frontex-coordinated Joint Operations. The focus of Analytics is the management of collected data and supporting analysts with data and analytical services.

Operational Analysis

In addition to creating a wider picture of the main trends in irregular migration and other phenomena in the medium and long term, Frontex also pays close attention to the daily developments in the areas of its joint operations at the external borders. Operational personnel made available by the Member States report back continuously via coordination centres on changes in the methods used of the people smugglers and other factors affecting joint operations. Smuggling networks pay close attention to operational activities at the border and adjust their tactics. For this reason, information such as the main nationalities of migrants, the routes they have taken and other details about the smuggling networks involved are all collected and analysed in order to maximise the effectiveness of operations.

This process already begins before a joint operation is launched. A specific assessment is drafted for the preparation of the planning of all operations describing the main trends, routes and methods used by smugglers for the key regions mostly targeted by smuggling networks. This assessment points to where joint operations should be launched, for which period and what should be their focus. When a specific operation in set to be launched, the operational analysts focus on a higher level of details on the most likely routes used by people smugglers, their likely methods and other specific phenomena at local level. These details are then incorporated into a tactical focused assessment (TFA), which in turn is used to finalise the operational plan to determine exactly what types of technical equipment are most appropriate for a given operation. For example, it would show whether to use fast boats or larger vessels or whether helicopters or airplanes would be best suited to a given environment. The precise location and length of joint operations are also determined largely by the TFA.

All this intelligence is then fed back to operational personnel via international, national and local coordination centres to constantly refine the daily operational procedures to maximise effectiveness.

The Eurosur Regulation requires Frontex to assess the impact of migration and cross border crime on all sea and land sections at the external border of the Member States of the European Union. This task is carried out by operational analysts who regularly look at the factors that influence the level of threat, vulnerability and impact on each of the sections.

Operational analysis yields a great number of periodic reports that provide a fresh and detailed picture not only for operational personnel but also for Frontex management, the European Commission and national and international law enforcement bodies. All the data gathered through operational analysis are also used in the strategic analysis process to keep the situational picture as up-to-date as possible.

Analytics

The Analytics Sectors was established to expand the Risk Analysis Unit's data and geo analysis capabilities and to sustain the high quality level of knowledge delivered and managed by it. The sector consists of two teams supporting the Strategic and Operational Sectors in their ad-hoc and bespoke exploitation of data and intelligence (Data Team) and through the provision and development of geospatial services (GIS Team).

The risk analysis approach to analytics is human-centric. People are behind the collected data, are analysing it, and are taking decisions based on it. The recognition of patterns in the data, the improvement of the analysts' experience via analytics, as well as the integration of the geographical context to the gained knowledge are aimed at supporting decision makers in the understanding of their critical business decision. Analytics supports in identifying the additional pieces of information that help managers improve the quality of their decisions.

The coordination of the Data Management cycle carried out by the Data Team aims at facilitating the introduction into the intelligence cycle of the processes, policies and solutions to govern, protect, maintain and use of existing and new Risk Analysis-managed datasets. This Data Management cycle also includes developments in the areas of data discovery, data integration and aggregation as well as data insight (extraction of value and knowledge based on advanced analytics). The GIS Team is responsible for the implementation of collaborative interface enabling the embedding of GIS Analytical Service Areas for the user-level management of statistical and operational geo-data.

The provision of geospatial intelligence through tailored products and services goes significantly beyond the usual imagery used for its elaboration and requires a thorough understanding of the complexity of the operational environment and the delivery of innovative geospatial solutions tailored to the analysts' needs.

Vulnerability Assessment

One of the core elements of the new Regulation is that the Agency is now also tasked to carry out vulnerability assessments on Member States' capacity to manage their borders. Vulnerability assessments help to contribute to an efficient, high and uniform level of border control at the external borders of the EU. They enable to identify and subsequently propose measures to eliminate any eventual weaknesses and thus serve also the purpose of preventing crisis at the EU external borders.

According to the Regulation, the Agency should monitor and assess the availability of the Member States' technical equipment, systems, capabilities, resources, infrastructure and adequately skilled and trained staff necessary for border control. The scope of the vulnerability assessment is broad and allows for potential vulnerabilities to be identified in a wide range of areas related to border management capacities.

The methodology, which Frontex has established in close consultation with Member States and the Commission, is based on four overarching principles. Firstly, it provides for the engagement of Member States to ensure ownership of the results and consistent application. Secondly, vulnerabilities are assessed by – on a continuous basis - taking into account, apart from the available technical and human resources capacity, the type and level of threats to which Member States are exposed and their impact. As the methodology is founded on (regularly changing) EU risks, this principle also allows for a clear distinction from the Schengen Evaluation Mechanism. Thirdly, it adopts a future-oriented approach so that the implementation of recommendations can prevent the development of crises. Finally, it does not seek to establish a mere checklist of available capacities but focuses on the analysis of data collected from a wide range of sources, so that the actual mobilisation of these capacities can be assessed.

The vulnerability assessment methodology is structured around one single overall process resulting in annual baseline assessments. These assessments are complemented with specific assessments stimulated by the identification of upcoming challenges, the monitoring of the situation along the external borders and the assessment of Member States' contributions to the rapid reaction pool.

Roles & Responsibilities

Schengen countries are obliged to deploy sufficient staff and resources to ensure a "high and uniform level of control" at their external borders. They must ensure that border guards are properly trained. EU and Schengen Associated Countries also assist each other in the effective application of border controls via operational cooperation, which is coordinated by Frontex, the European Border and Coast Guard Agency.

The Schengen area now extends along some 44 000 km of external sea borders and almost 9 000 km of land borders. It comprises 26 countries (including a number of non-EU states, so-called Schengen Associated Countries), meaning free movement for nearly half a billion people inside the Schengen area in exchange for strict controls at external borders. Simply put, the Schengen area's external border is only as strong as its weakest link.

The Schengen Borders Code governs the crossing of the external border, facilitating access for those who have a legitimate interest to enter into the EU and tightening security at the EU's external frontiers for those, who have no right to enter or stay. It clearly states that the primary responsibility of border control lies with those Schengen countries that have an external border –land and sea borders and international airports. They must ensure that proper checks and effective surveillance are carried out there.

Frontex's mission is to promote, coordinate and develop European Border Management in line with the EU fundamental rights charter and the concept of EU-integrated border management.

Frontex also provides technical and operational assistance to Member States through joint operations and rapid border interventions, as well as technical and operational assistance in the support of search and rescue operations at sea and organises. In addition, Frontex coordinates and conducts return operations and assists EU countries in raising and harmonising border management standards to help combat cross-border crime.

How it works

While regular border control is the exclusive responsibility of the Member States, Frontex's operational role focuses on coordination of deployment of additional experts and technical equipment to those border areas which find themselves under significant pressure. Frontex also builds the capacity of the Member States in various areas related to border control, including training and sharing of best practices.

Intelligence-driven

Frontex joint operations are planned and developed on the basis of an Annual Risk Analysis Reports which analyses the likely future risk of irregular migration and cross-border crime along the EU external border. During the annual meetings with Member States the agency prioritises the proposed joint operations on the basis of their importance and the resources available in order to ensure an effective response.

Consultation with Member States

Together with the host country Frontex makes an assessment of the number of officers with specific expertise and the quantity and type of technical equipment required. Frontex then directs a request to all

Member States and Schengen Associated Countries for the necessary officers, clearly specifying their required profiles (including document experts, border checks, surveillance experts, dog handlers) as well as specific equipment needed for the operation (such as helicopters, planes, patrol cars, thermo-vision equipment, heart-beat detectors). Those countries then decide on the level of contribution they can make to the joint operation.

Operational Plan

This document clearly defines the aim of each joint operation, where it is to take place and the quantities and types of technical equipment and officers to take part. Many operations require the deployment of debriefing officers, who conduct interviews with migrants with the purpose of gathering information about people-smuggling networks. In addition, cultural mediators and interpreters enable migrants to express themselves in their own languages. The operational plan also clearly states the rules of engagement for officers taking part in the operation.

Implementation

At this stage, border guards and technical equipment are deployed to the operational area to carry out their duties according to the operational plan. The deployed officers (known as guest officers) work under the command and control of the authorities of the country hosting the operation.

During deployment, guest officers may perform all tasks and exercise all powers for border checks or border surveillance in accordance with Schengen Borders Code. These tasks include border checks, border surveillance, stamping, interviewing undocumented persons, consultation of databases.

Guest officers wear their national uniforms and a blue armband (picture) with the insignia of the EU and Frontex. For the purposes of identification vis-à-vis national authorities and citizens, guest officers carry an accreditation document, provided by Frontex, which they must present on request.

Code of conduct

All officers deployed to an operation coordinated by the agency are bound by the Frontex Code of Conduct, which includes specific provisions on the respect of fundamental rights and the right to international protection. It lays out a set of behavioural standards that all staff involved in a Frontex joint operation must follow.

Evaluation

Once completed, each operation is evaluated by Frontex, the participating countries and other stakeholders involved ensuring that the operational process is constantly refined.

General

Frontex Joint Operations take place at three types of border – sea, land and air. Each operation is based on risk analysis and uniquely tailored to the circumstances identified by the agency in one of its risk analysis products.

Sea

As with all border control, sea border activities are divided into border checks (conducted at the border crossing points at sea ports) and border surveillance, which is conducted at sea. Frontex, the European Border and Coast Guard Agency, coordinated joint operations at sea represent Europe's biggest search and rescue operation. Every year thousands of migrants attempt to reach the EU by sea, often travelling in dangerously over-crowded and unseaworthy boats.

International law obliges all vessels to provide assistance to any persons found in distress, making search and rescue a priority for everyone operating at sea. Frontex's role in search and rescue operations is enshrined in its Regulation. Frontex is obliged to provide technical and operational assistance to Member States and non-EU countries in support of such operations that may arise during border surveillance operations at sea.

Search and rescue is a specific objective of the operational plan of every Frontex sea operation. It is important to underline that these operations are always coordinated by the national Maritime Rescue Coordination Centres (MRCC), which orders vessels that are either the closest to the incident or the most capable ones to assist in the rescue.

Officers deployed by Frontex at the border crossing points at sea ports play an important role in helping conduct border checks and assist in the registration process of irregular migrants. They help national authorities in collecting finger prints and determine the nationality of migrants during screening interviews. Some of them also gather information about the criminal networks involved in people smuggling and trafficking.

Land

Border checks are conducted at border crossing points set up at road and rail points of entry to the EU. In addition to these checks, border guards deployed in Frontex operations conduct border surveillance along land borders.

More than 3,500 km of land borders run along the EU's eastern frontier, from the Arctic circle in northern Finland to the Evros river region of Greece. Monitoring the migratory flows and reacting accordingly to changing trends at these diverse land borders is a constant challenge. Enhancing the effectiveness of overall border control measures, as well as maximising surveillance and situational awareness by focussing efforts at precise points of increased pressure, are all part of running land border operations.

Frontex also helps ensure a constant exchange of expertise and experience among national border guard officers. The range of skills used at the land borders varies from detection of persons hidden in vehicles at border crossing points to patrols with dogs or night vision observation. In so-called "second-line" activities expertise covers detection of falsified documents or interviewing undocumented persons to determine their nationality.

As with all Frontex operational activities land operations are based on risk analysis reports and when a need is identified, operations are generally run in phases with the duration, place and time being determined close to implementation.

Frontex also has goals for future development concerning land borders. One of these is increased cooperation with customs authorities. Frontex actively participates in information sharing and other integration activities with the Customs Cooperation Working Party (CCWP) and has been involved in increasing cooperation between border-control authorities and customs as well as with national and EU authorities, the Commission and the European Ant-Fraud office (OLAF).

Air

Joint Operations at airports present unique challenges. The point of entry is usually a passport-control booth and hardly anybody can enter undetected. For this reason alone, international airports represent a specific range of border management issues.

The methods used by irregular migrants are also different at airports. Some people intending to stay illegally in the EU use false documents or well-practised techniques under the supervision of criminal facilitators to deceive border officers. And then there are the sheer numbers. According to the Frontex risk analysis, as many as 45% of Europe's 271 million entry/exits per year are from countries "at risk" of being an irregular migration source. If only 1 percent of these 121 million passengers are migrating irregularly, that means as many as 1.2

million irregular migrants could enter the EU every year through its airports.

But air border operations are about more than passport control. Activities before, during and after passport control are essential to ensuring a secure border. This includes constant information-gathering and analysis of methods used by criminals and other intelligence, effective information exchange between airports, airlines and Member States, specialist officer training and the use of cutting edge technology to detect forged documents and other deceptions.

Frontex has established a reliable system of information gathering, analysis and exchange with Europol and other partners. Frontex receives up-to-date information from more than 130 airports and provides a weekly European overview of the situation at Europe's external air borders, along with as rapid alerts on new trends and false documents.

Return

Frontex, the European Border and Coast Guard Agency, has become an essential actor in migration enforcement on the European level, taking on new responsibilities and tools related to returns of people who have exhausted all legal avenues to legitimise their stay within the EU. This has led to a significant rise in the number of foreign nationals Frontex has helped EU countries to return in recent years. In 2017, the figure surpassed 13 000, more than double the number from the previous year. This compares with 3 500 people returned by the agency in 2015.

Frontex is responsible for the coordination of return operations at a technical and operational level, including voluntary departures. In practice, this means that Frontex offers support in the organisation and implementation, including financing or co-financing, of return operations organised from individual Member States

Where does Frontex come in?

Non-EU nationals who have exhausted all legal avenues to remain in the EU or who have committed offences in a Member State, receive a return decision from a court or competent authorities of Member States. According to Eurostat, every year around a quarter of a million people are subject to such orders. The vast majority of them leave voluntarily. However, when illegally-staying non-EU nationals refuse to comply with the return decision, as a last resort they may be forcibly returned.

Frontex can assist Member States upon their request or on the agency's proposal in carrying out return operations through:

1.   organising or coordinating both national and joint return operation;

2.   assisting Member States in both forced return operations and in voluntary departures;

3.   organising or coordinating collecting return operations.

Frontex is responsible for the coordination of return operations, but it is crucial to understand that the decision about who should be returned is always taken by the judicial or administrative authorities of the Member States. According to European legislation, the individual is always given the possibility to appeal against this return decision. Frontex does not enter into the merits of return decisions issued by the Member States. This is the exclusive responsibility of Member States.

Types of operations

Forced return operations, voluntary departures and readmissions

While Frontex continues to coordinate **forced return operations** from individual Member States, it may also propose to coordinate or organise **returns on its own initiative**, also by chartering of aircraft. In addition, Frontex provides support with **voluntary**

departures of non-EU nationals who are subject to individual return decisions with a granted period for voluntary departure.

The agency can also provide support to Member States in **readmission operations** by providing transportation and escort officers to Member States.

Joint return operations

Most Member States organise return operations individually. There is, however, a possibility for two or more countries to organise a **joint return operation.** If one Member State organises a return operation by air to a specific country of return and has some spare capacity on the plane, it can invite other Member States to take part. The organising Member State informs Frontex about its intention to conduct a return flight and requests the assistance of Frontex to coordinate this operation. Frontex then dispatches this information to all other Member States.

The returnees are accompanied by escort officers from the different Member States taking part in the operation, medical staff and translators. Member States shall monitor every return operation in accordance with EU legislation.

Collecting return operations

Frontex can also coordinate **collecting return operations**, where the means of transport and escort officers are provided by the non-EU country of destination.

The returnees from the participating Member States are transported to the organising Member State. The participating Member States and the agency ensure that the respect for fundamental rights, the principle of *non-refoulement,* and the proportionate use of means of constraints are guaranteed during the entire return operation.

Prior to organising collecting return operations, the escorts of the non-EU country of return are trained by the agency to comply with EU standards, including on fundamental rights. In addition, at least one Member State representative, one forced-return monitor and medical staff are present throughout the entire return operation.

Pools of return experts

As part of the new expanded mandate on returns, Frontex has created three pools of return experts who support the return of non-EU nationals from Member States: return monitors, return escorts and return specialists. The experts nominated by Member States are at the disposal of Frontex and may be deployed to a host Member State at its request.

These experts will be deployed in return operations or return interventions coordinated by the agency to carry out specific tasks, such as assisting in the acquisition of travel documents from non-EU countries and facilitation of consular cooperation, or in order to provide the Member States with additional resources to escort returnees, as well as to comply with their obligation to monitor forced return operations. Some of the experts have specific expertise in child protection.

Monitoring of return operations

All return operations must be monitored in accordance with EU law and a forced-return monitor must deliver a report to the agency and to all the Member States involved in the given operation. The monitoring covers the whole return operation, from the pre-departure phase to the hand-over of the returnees in the non-EU country of return.

Other return-related activities

Frontex plays a role in *coordinating return-related activities* of Member States. In addition, the agency coordinates the use of IT systems and activities that enable the exchange of information between Member States in return matters.

The agency supports and facilitates cooperation between Member States and non-EU countries in the field of identification – establishing nationality, acquiring travel documents and by providing practical information on countries of return. Those Member States which experience particular challenges related to their return systems receive specific technical and operational assistance, based on clearly identified needs..

The Return Process

The return process consists of a number of steps:

- **Voluntary return:** The national authorities inform all returnees about the possibility of assisted voluntary return. About half of those eligible for return accept that this option.

- **The Return decision:** Individuals who have exhausted all legal avenues to legitimise their stay within the EU or who have committed offences in a Member State receive a return decision from a court or competent authorities of Member States. These decisions are taken by the relevant authorities in Member States on individual assessment.

- **Appeals procedure:** Every person has the right to appeal against the return decision. This process is **in the hands of the authorities of the individual Member States**.

- **Voluntary departure:** Non-EU nationals subject to individual return decisions may be granted a period for voluntary departure.

- **Identification process**: Non-EU nationals without proper travel documents cannot be returned. The non-EU country authorities have to officially confirm their nationality in order to be able to issue travel documents. Frontex can assist the Member States national authorities with the process of identification.

- **Acquisition of travel documents**: Once the authorities of the non-EU country establishes that the national is indeed from their country, they can issue a travel document. In case a travel document is not issued by the relevant authorities, a European travel document could be issued by Member States based on an agreement signed with the country of return.

- **The Return operation:** The returns are carried out by Member States by, land, sea or air, although mostly by commercial flights. Some return operations are also carried out by chartered flights, either unilaterally or jointly by Member States. The use of a charter is only possible with the consent of each country of return. Joint return operations are usually coordinated and co-financed by Frontex.

- **Acceptance by the country of return:** A return operation is complete upon the successful handover of a returnee to the authorities of the country of return. If the handover is rejected, the returnee is transferred back to the Member State that first requested the return.

Rapid Intervention

A rapid border intervention is designed to bring immediate assistance to a Member State that is under urgent and exceptional pressure at its external border, especially related to large numbers of non-EU nationals trying to enter the territory of a Member State illegally.

The interventions rely on the rapid reaction pools of 1500 officers and equipment from Member States, which are required to provide them – officers and staff within five days and equipment within 10 days.

Deployment Procedure

A Member State starts the procedure to launch a rapid border intervention by requesting one, along with providing a description of the situation, possible aims and its needs. The Frontex Executive Director may send experts to assess the situation and immediately informs the

Management Board of the agency about the request. The Executive Director must decide within two working days whether to launch the rapid intervention, notifying the requesting Member State and the Management Board of his decision.

The Executive Director and the Member State then have to draw up an operational plan within three days after a decision to launch a rapid border intervention. As soon as the plan is agreed, Frontex asks other Member States to immediately provide border guards and other relevant staff from the rapid reaction pool, indicating the relevant profiles and numbers of officers from each. They should be deployed within five days. Member States may also be asked to provide additional officers, who would be provided within additional seven days.

Command

Members of the teams may perform tasks and exercise powers under instructions from and in the presence of border guards of the Member State requesting assistance.

Frontex Executive Director appoints a coordinating officer to act as an interface between the agency and the other authorities involved, monitoring the correct implementation of the operational plan.

Search & Rescue

International law obliges all vessels to provide assistance to any persons found in distress, making search and rescue (SAR) a priority for everyone operating at sea.

Frontex's role in SAR operations is enshrined in its Regulation 2016/1624. Frontex is obliged to provide technical and operational assistance to Member States and non-EU countries in support of SAR operations that may arise during border surveillance operations at sea.

SAR is a specific objective of the operational plan of every Frontex joint maritime operation. For this reason, vessels deployed by

Frontex to an operational area are always ready to also provide support to the national authorities in SAR operations.

It is important to underline that SAR operations are always coordinated by the national Maritime Rescue Coordination Centres (MRCC). The MRCC orders vessels that are either the closest to the incident or the most capable ones (due to the specialised training of the crew, or the vessels specifications, etc.) to assist in the rescue. These may include national commercial or military vessels, vessels deployed by Frontex, private boats and other.

During a standard border control operation, Frontex-deployed vessels operate under the command of the International Coordination Centre (ICC), but when contacted by the Maritime Rescue Coordination Centre and redirected to a SAR operation, it is the MRCC that takes command. Once Frontex vessels reach people in distress, they first provide immediate medical assistance and give them food and water. Once a rescue operation is completed, migrants are disembarked and handed over to the national authorities for identification and registration. In Italy and Greece, Frontex officers assist in registration and identification of migrants arriving in hotspots.

6. European Union Agency for the Operational Management of Large-Scale IT Systems in the Area of Freedom, Security and Justice (eu-LISA)

The European Union Agency for the Operational Management of Large-Scale IT Systems in the Area of Freedom, Security and Justice (eu-LISA), a newly established EU agency to provide a long-term solution for the operational management of large-scale IT systems, which are essential instruments in the implementation of the asylum, border management and migration policies of the EU.

The Agency is currently managing Eurodac, the second generation Schengen Information System (SIS II) and the Visa Information System (VIS).

The SIS II database permits the sharing of information on criminal matters to make sure the coordinated investigation of crimes that no longer respect national borders. The VIS system, ensures fair, efficient and secure processing of the visa application processes and border entry travel procedures of external visitors to EU while the Eurodac system permits the monitoring of asylum applications from those who may need protection under EU values and norms.

The Agency was established in 2011 (Establishing Regulation (EU) No 1077/2011) and started its activities on 1 December 2012.

The headquarters of eu-LISA are in Tallinn, Estonia, whilst its operational centre is in Strasbourg, France. There is also a business continuity site for the systems under management based in Sankt Johann im Pongau, Austria and a Liaison Office in Brussels, Belgium.

The application of the Agency's mission allows it to achieve its overall vision, which is:

- To provide high-quality efficient services and solutions;

- To build trust amongst all stakeholders and continuously align the capabilities of technology with the evolving needs of the Member States;
- To grow as a centre of excellence.

Core Activities

eu-LISA is the European Agency responsible for the operational management of Eurodac, the Schengen Information System (SIS) and the Visa Information System (VIS). Recent legislation now sees the Agency also entrusted with the development and running of the European Entry/Exit System (EES), the European Travel Information Authorisation System (ETIAS) and the European Criminal Record Information System for Third Country Nationals (ECRIS-TCN).

Further to the evolution and development of individual systems, eu-LISA has been tasked with ensuring the interoperability of large-scale IT systems. Interoperability and its components will provide faster and more reliable data to both border management and law enforcement authorities, be they at a desk or out in the field.

In order to fulfil this mandate, the Agency must keep all IT systems under its responsibility functioning 24 hours a day, 7 days a week, to allow the continuous and uninterrupted exchange of data between the national authorities using them.

eu-LISA is also mandated to ensure that it applies the highest levels of information security and data protection to the information entrusted to it, ensuring that personal information is treated fairly, lawfully and correctly, in full compliance with the relevant data protection principles and legislation in force.

Additional products and services that the Agency provides include:

Participation in preparatory processes to design, develop and implement new systems, including execution of pilot projects;

Training: provision of bespoke system training plans for national authorities on technical use of IT systems managed by the Agency;

Reporting and statistics: timely and accurate provision of statistics and information on the performance of the systems as foreseen in the relevant legal bases and the fulfilment of all reporting obligations laid down in the Establishing Regulation and legal bases for the IT systems under the Agency's management.

7. Types of large-scale information systems in the area of freedom, security and justice

7.1. Existing large - scale information systems in the field of freedom, security and justice

7.1.1. Schengen Information System (SIS)

The Schengen Information System (SIS) is a large-scale IT system that supports public security and the exchange of information on people and objects between national law enforcement authorities, border controls, customs, visa and judicial authorities.

As people and goods can move in the Schengen area without being checked at internal borders, the SIS is used by security officers to help people be safe and fight cross-border crime.

The SIS supports Europe's internal security authorities in compliance with data protection requirements.

At the end of 2018, the SIS contained over 82.2 million alerts and over 267,000 alert "visits" were registered. Statistics show that in 2018, the SIS was searched for more than 6.1 billion times by all Member States, 1 billion times more (ie 20% more) than in 2017.

After two years of intensive efforts, in early 2018 eu-LISA successfully launched the automated fingerprint identification platform SIS (AFIS). SIS AFIS responds to the requests of the European law enforcement community to have an advanced tool at EU level that allows the identification of those who are of interest only through fingerprints.

The SIS reform package, the legislation for which was adopted in December 2018, introduced technical and operational improvements to the system (such as the introduction of additional alert categories and the expansion of the list of sites for which alerts can be issued) in order to further strengthening the operational efficiency and effectiveness of the SIS. eu-LISA, as the operational manager of the system, is progressing in a similar way, using its skills and capabilities to further develop the Schengen cooperation.

Architecture

The SIS consists of:

• Central system (Central SIS) with

• a technical support function (CS-SIS), containing a database (SIS database) performing technical supervision and administrative tasks, and a backup CS-SIS;

• a single national interface (NI-SIS) in each country, which members use to enter, update, delete and search SIS data;

• a national system (N.SIS) in each country for communication with the Central SIS, including at least one national or shared N.SIS. It is not possible to search for data files in another N.SIS unless the countries concerned agree to share the file;

• The communication infrastructure between the CS-SIS, the back-up CS-SCO and the NI-SIS provides an encrypted virtual network for the SIS data and their exchange between the SIRENE bureaux.

The European Union Agency for the Operational Management of Large-Scale Information Systems in the Area of Freedom, Security and Justice (eu-LISA):

• implement technical solutions to strengthen the continuous availability of the SIS;

• in exceptional circumstances, develop an additional copy of the SIS database;

• must submit a report no later than 28 December 2019 on the possibilities for technical solutions, containing an independent impact assessment and cost-benefit analysis;

• publishes a list of N.SIS national services and SIRENE bureaux.

The rules of procedure state that:

• alerts should remain in the SIS only as long as necessary for their specific purpose and be deleted when they reach it;

• alerts must be considered within certain periods. The Member State may then decide to extend them, otherwise the alerts are automatically deleted. The review periods are:

• 5 years: persons wanted for arrest for surrender or extradition and missing persons who may or may not be placed under protection,

• 3 years: persons sought for assistance in court proceedings and unknown wanted persons,

• 1 year: children at risk, vulnerable persons who need to be protected from travel and persons for discreet examination or specific checks,

• 10 years: objects for discreet investigation, specific inspections or for seizure or use as evidence in criminal proceedings;

• the categories of data to be entered into the system. They are designed to help end users make quick decisions. Include minimum requirements (surname, date of birth, reason for the signal and actions to be taken) and other data, such as type of violation, photographic and dactyloscopic information, if available;

• the use of biometric and dactyloscopic data must comply with EU law and fundamental rights and meet minimum quality standards and technical specifications;

• a case must be appropriate, relevant and sufficiently important to ensure an alert in the SIS, for example an alert related to a terrorist offense, meets these criteria;

• only the issuing Member State may modify, add, correct, update or delete data in the SIS;

• A State that considers that the action on an alert is incompatible with its national law, international obligations or essential interests may place a special restrictive sign on the alert. This shows that it will not take any action on its territory.

Costs:

• the EU budget covers the costs of operating, maintaining and developing the central SIS and the communication infrastructure;

• Schengen Member States cover the costs of operation, maintenance and development of their own N.SIS.

Categories of signals under each regulation

Regulation (EU) 2018/1860 strengthens the implementation of EU return policy and reduces incentives for illegal immigration into the EU:

• it sets out general conditions and procedures for the input and processing of alerts and for the exchange of additional information on third-country nationals subject to return decisions;

• it requires national authorities to enter alerts at the time of a return decision;

• it establishes a harmonized procedure for:

• the categories of data to be entered in the signal,

• verifying that a return decision has been complied with and, if not, the follow-up between the relevant authorities,

• withholding and deleting alerts to ensure that there is no delay between the departure of a third-country national and the activation of an entry ban,

• mandatory consultation between national authorities before

• granting or extending a residence permit or long-stay visa to a third-country national who may be subject to a return signal to another EU country

• Introducing an alert for a return decision if the person is staying illegally anywhere in the EU.

Regulation (EU) 2018/1861 covers the use of the SIS for entry bans and border checks:

• it sets out the conditions and procedures for entering and processing alerts and for exchanging additional information * for third-country nationals who have been refused entry or residence in the EU;

• introduces a harmonized procedure for:

• the categories of data to be entered in the signal,

• mandatory alert when a third-country national is denied entry or residence because it poses a security threat or is subject to a restrictive regime that prevents entry or passage through an EU country,

• third-country nationals with the right to free movement within the EU,

• mandatory consultation between national authorities before issuing or extending a residence permit or long-stay visa to a third-country national who has been denied the right to enter or reside in another EU country;

• it ensures that third-country nationals have the right to be informed in writing if they are the subject of an alert.

Regulation 2018/1862 improves and expands the use of the SIS for cooperation between the police and the judiciary:

• it establishes the conditions and procedures for entering and processing alerts in the SIS for persons and objects, as well as for the exchange of additional information and data in police and judicial cooperation in criminal matters;

• it covers alert procedures for:

• persons wanted for arrest, extradition or

• missing persons;

• vulnerable persons who must be prevented from traveling for their own protection or to prevent a threat to public order or security;

• children at risk, in particular abduction, trafficking or involvement in terrorism;

• persons who are sought to cooperate in court proceedings as witnesses or because they have been summoned in connection with criminal proceedings;

• unknown wanted persons, whose identity is being sought;

• discrete or specific inspections and investigations to prevent, detect, investigate or prosecute criminal offenses, enforce a criminal conviction or prevent threats to public security;

• items to be seized or used as evidence in criminal proceedings, especially easily identifiable items such as cars, boats, airplanes, firearms, identity documents and banknotes.

Right to data

Individuals have the right to:
• know whether their personal data is processed or not, for what purposes and under what conditions;
• lodge a complaint with a supervisory authority;
• correct inaccurate personal data without undue delay;
• delete personal data if their use is no longer necessary or has been illegally processed;
• take action to access, correct, delete, obtain information or indemnify for a signal that affects them;
• receive compensation from a Member State for any material or non-pecuniary damage they suffer from the unlawful processing of their personal data.

The governments of the SIS members shall:
• are obliged to apply the rules on data protection rights;
• report annually to the European Data Protection Board on the number of requests for access to data and correction of inaccuracies received, as well as on the volume of court cases and their outcome.

Independent supervisory authorities shall control the lawfulness of the national processing of personal data in the SIS; The European Data Protection Supervisor, established under Regulation (EU) 2018/1725, plays the same role for eu-LISA. They shall cooperate in order to ensure the coordination of SIS supervision.

• Data processed in the SIS and related additional information may not be transmitted or made available to third countries or international organizations.

• Regulation (EU) 2018/1725 applies to personal data processed by eu-LISA, the European Border and Coast Guard Agency and Eurojust.

• Regulation (EU) 2016/679 and Directive (EC) 2016/680 apply to personal data processed by national competent authorities and services.

The following shall have access to the SIS data:

• National authorities responsible for:

• border control, police and customs checks;

• the prevention, detection, investigation or prosecution of terrorist acts or other serious criminal offenses;

• decisions, including on residence permits and long-stay visas, on the entry, stay and return of third-country nationals;

• security checks on third-country nationals applying for international protection;

• naturalization decisions;

• the prosecution in criminal proceedings and judicial investigations;

• the issuance of registration certificates for vehicles, boats, aircraft and firearms;

• The EU agencies below have the right to access and search the SIS data they need to carry out their responsibilities. They shall inform the issuing Member State when an alert is detected in a search. They cannot connect parts of the SIS or transmit any data to their own system.

• Europol: has access to all data, not just some as before. SIS Member States must inform the law enforcement authority of any findings or alerts related to terrorist offenses;

• Eurojust, which deals with judicial cooperation in criminal matters;

• European Border and Coast Guard teams involved in return tasks, as well as migration management assistance teams.

Every 5 years, the European Commission evaluates the use of SIS by these services.

Responsibilities

Each SIS Member State shall:

• ensures that the data are accurate, up-to-date and are entered and stored in the SIS in a lawful manner and that the general rules for data processing are complied with;

• creates, uses, maintains and develops its N.SIS in accordance with the common standards, protocols and technical procedures and connects it to NI-SIS;

• guarantees uninterrupted access of end-users to SIS data;

• transmits its signals through its N.SIS;

• appoint a N.SIS service with central responsibility for ensuring the smooth operation and security of its N.SIS, access of the competent authorities to the SIS, full compliance with the Regulation and appropriate availability of the SIS for all end-users;

• appoints a national authority (SIRENE bureau) as a single point of contact, acting 24 hours a day, 7 days a week to exchange and access all additional information on alerts and to facilitate follow-up;

• adopts security, business continuity and disaster recovery plans to protect data and prevent unauthorized access;

• apply rules of professional secrecy and confidentiality, including close monitoring of external contractors. Private companies and organizations have a ban on operational management of N.SIS;

• maintains electronic registers, which are usually deleted after 3 years, of alerts, access and exchange of personal data to verify that the search is lawful and to ensure the integrity and security of the data;

• Operates a national training program for SIS personnel with access to the SIS on data security, fundamental rights, including data protection rules and regulations.

The Commission:

• adopt implementing acts and delegated acts concerning the technical aspects of the SIS and update them as necessary;

• According to Regulation (EU) № 1053/2013, has a common coordinating role for the evaluation and monitoring mechanism it implements with EU governments to ensure full compliance with Schengen provisions at national level. This includes SIS assessment;

• report to the European Parliament and EU governments by 28 December 2019 and each year thereafter until it decides on the date of the start of SIS operations, on the state of preparations for the full implementation of the updated Regulation 2018/1862 on SIS;

• carry out a comprehensive assessment of the Central SIS, the exchange of additional information between national authorities, including an assessment of the Automated Fingerprint Identification System (AFIS) and SIS information campaigns, 3 years after the entry into force of the Regulation and every 4 years thereafter.

eu-LISA is responsible for:

• the Central SIS: its operational management, including quality checks on the data it contains and all the tasks necessary to ensure its operation 24 hours a day, seven days a year;

• communication infrastructure: key aspects, in particular supervision, security, coordination between Member States and suppliers, as well as budgetary and contractual issues;

• SIRENE bureaux: coordinating, managing and supporting the testing activities, maintaining and updating the technical specifications on the exchange of additional information between the bureaus and the communication infrastructure and managing technical changes;

• adopting the necessary measures to protect data and prevent unauthorized access or use, including security, business continuity and disaster recovery plans for the Central SIS and the Communication Infrastructure;

• application of rules on professional secrecy and confidentiality and maintenance of electronic registers under the same conditions as national authorities;

• making publicly available through the Official Journal of the EU a list of national authorities empowered to search SIS data;

• preparation of daily, monthly and annual statistics on the number of records by category of signals, omitting any personal data. Her reports are public.

Information campaign

• The Commission, in cooperation with the supervisory authorities and the European Data Protection Supervisor, leads the campaign. It starts when the legislation enters into force and is repeated at regular intervals in order to inform the public about:

• the objectives of the SIS;

• the data in it;
• the authorities that have access to them;
• data rights of individuals.
• The Commission maintains a publicly accessible website with all relevant SIS information.
• EU countries working with their supervisors need to inform the public about the SIS.

HOW LONG HAVE THE REGULATIONS APPLIED?

They are being implemented gradually and will generally be fully operational by 28 December 2021 at the latest. The date is to be set by the Commission after confirming that the following conditions are met:
• the implementing acts have been adopted;
• the national authorities have taken the necessary measures to process the data in the SIS and exchange additional information;
• eu-LISA has successfully met all its test requirements.
GENERAL INFORMATION
• Although based on different pieces of legislation, the SIS is a single system for sharing data and requests between its members.
• It is the most widely used and largest system for sharing information on security and border management in Europe. In 2018, it contained 82.2 million records, was accessed more than 6.1 billion times and had 267,239 results.
• It operates in 30 European countries: all EU members except Cyprus and Ireland, as well as in Iceland, Liechtenstein, Norway and Switzerland.

BASIC CONCEPTS

Alert: a set of data that enables authorities to identify a person or object and take appropriate action.
Fingerprint data: palm and fingerprint data.
Special restriction sign: termination of the signal at national level.

Return decisions: a judicial or administrative decision for a third-country national who is considered to be staying illegally and must return to his or her home country.

Additional information: information which is not part of the SIS alert data but is related to it.

7.1.2. Visa Information System (VIS)

Regulation (EC) № 767/2008 on the VIS defines the purpose and functionalities as well as the responsibilities for the Visa Information System (VIS). It provides the conditions and procedures for the exchange of visa data between the countries of the European Union (EU) and the associated countries applying the common visa policy. This facilitates the processing of applications for short-stay visas and decisions on extension, cancellation and cancellation of visas, as well as visa checks and checks and identifications of applicants and visa holders.

The purpose of the Visa Information System (VIS) is to improve the implementation of the common visa policy, consular cooperation and consultations between central visa authorities by:
• facilitating the visa application procedure;
• prevention of visa shopping;
• facilitating the fight against fraud;
• facilitating checks at external border crossings and national territories;
• assisting in the identification of persons who do not meet the requirements for entry, residence or stay in the national territories;
• Facilitating the implementation of the Dublin II Regulation to designate the EU country responsible for examining the asylum application of a non-EU country and for examining this application;
• contributes to the prevention of threats to the internal security of EU countries.

n specific cases, national authorities and Europol may request access to data entered in the VIS in order to prevent, detect and investigate terrorist offenses and criminal offenses. The procedures for consultation in such circumstances are set out in Council Decision 2008/633 / JHA. These consultations shall be carried out through central access points in the participating countries and by Europol, which shall verify the requests and ensure compliance with the above decision.

Only the following categories of data shall be recorded in the VIS:

• alphanumeric data for the applicant and for the requested visas, issued, refused, annulled, revoked or extended;

• photos;

• data on fingerprints;

• links to previous visa applications and to the application documents of persons traveling together.

Access to VIS:

• for entering, modifying or deleting data is reserved exclusively for duly authorized staff of the visa authorities;

• for data consultation, is reserved exclusively for duly authorized staff of visa authorities and bodies responsible for external border checks, immigration checks and asylum and is limited to the extent to which the data are necessary for the performance of their tasks.

Authorities having access to the VIS must ensure that its use is limited to what is necessary, appropriate and proportionate for the performance of their tasks. In addition, they should ensure that visa applicants and visa holders are not discriminated against when using the VIS and that their human dignity and integrity are respected.

Entering data from visa authorities

Once the application has been declared admissible as specified in the Visa Code, the visa authority shall establish the dossier by entering in the VIS a set of data listed in this Regulation, such as personal travel data and travel data provided in the application form, photo and fingerprints.

When a visa decision is taken, the visa authority shall add other important information, including the type of visa, the territory in which the visa holder is entitled to travel, the period of validity, the number of authorized entries into the territory and the duration of the authorized stay.

Additional data must be entered if the visa authority representing another EU country suspends the examination of the application, as well as when a decision is taken to refuse, cancel or revoke a visa or to extend the validity of the visa.

Use of visa data and other competent authorities

The competent visa authority may consult the VIS to examine applications and decisions to issue, refuse, extend, cancel or revoke a visa or to shorten the period of validity of the visa. He is authorized to perform searches with some of the data included in the application form and the application file. If the search shows that the data on the applicant are stored in the VIS, the visa authority will be granted access to the application file and related application files.

For prior consultation, the State responsible for examining the application must send all VIS requests for consultation with the application number, indicating the State or Parties to be consulted. The VIS will forward the request to the State concerned, which in turn will send the reply to the VIS, which will then forward the reply to the requesting Party.

For statistical and reporting purposes, the visa authorities are empowered to consult data that do not allow the identification of the applicant.

The authorities responsible for carrying out checks at the external borders and within the national territories shall have access to the VIS search with the visa sticker number, together with fingerprints. They may search the VIS in order to verify the identity and / or authenticity of the visa and / or whether the person meets the requirements for entry, residence or stay in the national territories. If, on the basis of this search in the VIS, details of the visa holder are found, the relevant authorities may consult certain details in the application file.

To identify a person who may not be able or no longer meet the required conditions, the competent authorities shall have access to a fingerprint data search. If that person's fingerprints cannot be used or the fingerprint search fails, the relevant authorities may search the VIS with the name, sex, date and place of birth and / or information taken from the document. for traveling. They can be used in combination with the nationality of the person.

Migration services have access to a search in the VIS with fingerprint data, but only for the purpose of determining the EU country responsible for examining an asylum application and for examining an asylum application. However, if the asylum seeker's fingerprints cannot be used or the search fails, the authorities may carry out the search with the data provided above.

Each application file is stored in the VIS for a maximum of five years. Only the responsible State has the right to change or delete the data it has transmitted to the VIS.

Work and responsibilities

Following a transitional period when the Commission was responsible, from 1 December 2012 the European Agency for the Operational Management of Large-Scale Information Systems in the Area of Freedom, Security and Justice (euLISA) was responsible for the operational management of the Central VIS and national interfaces. In addition, by providing a communication infrastructure between the two, euLISA is responsible for the supervision, security and coordination of the relationship between the parties involved and the service provider. euLISA also ensures that the VIS is operated in accordance with the VIS Regulation and that only duly authorized staff have access to the data processed in the VIS.

The VIS is connected to each country's national system through the country's national interface. Participating Parties shall designate a national authority that is connected to the national interfaces and that provides access to the VIS by the relevant authorities.

Each country is responsible for:

• the development, organization, management, operation and maintenance of its national system;

• ensuring the security of the data before and during the transmission of their national interface and for this purpose adoption of a security plan;

• the management and conditions of access by duly authorized staff of the competent national authorities to the VIS in accordance with this Regulation;

• bearing the costs incurred by its national system.

VIS data shall not be provided to third countries or international organizations, unless they are necessary to verify the identity of a third-country national in individual cases. The communication may be made when a set of conditions are met, with due regard for the rights of refugees and persons seeking international protection.

Data protection

The responsible State shall provide the data subjects with the identity and contact details of the controller responsible for processing the data, the purposes for which the data are processed in the VIS, the categories of data recipients, the data retention period and the right of access, rectification and erasure. of the data. In addition, the party must inform stakeholders of its obligation to collect the data. Every person has the right to receive information on how to bring a case or complaint before the competent authorities or courts of the respective country if he is denied the right of access or the right to rectify or delete data relating to him.

Each EU country must require a national supervisory authority set up in accordance with Directive 95/46 / EC to monitor the lawfulness of that person's processing of personal data. The European Data Protection Supervisor shall monitor the activities of euLISA.

Start of operations

The VIS became operational following the technical implementation of the Central VIS, the national interfaces and the communication infrastructure and completed a comprehensive VIS test. The parties also had to take certain necessary steps to collect and transmit data in the first region, followed by gradual introduction in other regions.

As a Schengen instrument, this Regulation applies to EU countries with the exception of the United Kingdom and Ireland. Denmark has decided to implement the regulation, which also applies to Iceland, Norway and Switzerland.

The Schengen consultation network (VISION) is currently used as a communication network for visa consultations. Once the VIS is operational, the VIS Mail mechanism can be used in parallel to transmit messages:

• related to consular cooperation;

• in connection with requests for any supporting documents related to an application;

• indicates that inaccurate data have been processed in the VIS;

• indicating that the applicant has acquired the citizenship of an EU country.

Once all Schengen visa publications are linked to the VIS, the VIS Mail mechanism is the only communication network for the exchange of messages via the VIS.

7.1.3. European System for the Comparison of Fingerprints of Asylum Seekers (Eurodac)

The Eurodac system was originally set up in 2000 (Regulation (EC) № 2725/2000) and has been operational since 2003. The European Commission considers it to be a very successful IT tool.

The original legislation on Eurodac (Council Regulation (EU) № 2725/2000) did not provide for the possibility for law enforcement authorities to require a comparison of data. However, the new regulation allows the national police and Europol to compare fingerprints related to criminal investigations with those contained in Eurodac. The new regulation extends the Eurodac system, which is an EU-wide biometric database containing fingerprints of asylum seekers and non-EU / EEA nationals for comparison between EU countries.

The aim is:

• make it easier for EU countries to determine the responsibility for examining an asylum application by comparing the fingerprints of applicants asylum application, and for non-EU / EEA nationals with a central database; and

• to allow law enforcement authorities, under strict conditions, to consult Eurodac in order to investigate, detect and prevent terrorist acts or serious crimes.

Due to the fundamental right to privacy, law enforcement agencies have the right to use Eurodac for comparisons:

• only if there are serious grounds that such a comparison will significantly help them to prevent, detect or investigate a terrorist or other serious crime; and

• only as a last resort, after several other checks have been carried out.

The data contained in Eurodac should not be shared with non-EU countries.

Some asylum seekers, non-EU / EEA nationals or stateless persons refuse to cooperate with EU Member States' attempts to take their fingerprints in order to include them in the Eurodac database. In this regard, the European Commission has issued a document on best possible practices related to fingerprinting.

Each EU country must take the fingerprints of all asylum seekers and persons detained in an attempt to cross the border illegally (eg non-EU / EEA nationals and stateless persons who enter without valid documents) over the age of 14 and must transmit the data to Eurodac within 72 hours.

When it is established that an asylum seeker or a citizen of a non-EU / EEA country is residing illegally in an EU country, then that EU country can consult Eurodac to check whether the person has previously applied for asylum in an EU country or whether he has ever been detained in an attempt to enter the EU illegally.

Fingerprint data must be deleted once asylum seekers, non-EU / EEA nationals or stateless persons have acquired EU citizenship.

This Regulation helps to implement the Dublin III Regulation (Regulation (EU) № 604/2013), which lays down rules for determining the EU country responsible for examining an asylum application.

System structure and basic principles

Eurodac consists of:
and a central computer database for fingerprints ("central system"), consisting of:
 • central unit,
 • plan and system for ensuring continuity of activity;
 • a communication infrastructure between the central system and the Member States, which provides an encrypted virtual network dedicated to Eurodac data ("communication infrastructure").

Each Member State shall have a single national access point. Data on persons processed by the Central System shall be processed on behalf of the home Member State under the conditions laid down in this Regulation and shall be separated by appropriate technical means. The Eurodac rules also apply to activities carried out by Member States from the transmission of the data to the Central System to the use of the results of their comparison. The procedure for taking fingerprints shall be determined and applied in accordance with the national practice of the Member State concerned and in compliance with the guarantees provided for in the Charter of Fundamental Rights of the European Union, the Convention for the Protection of Human Rights and Fundamental Freedoms and the Convention. United Nations Organization for the Rights of the Child.

Operational management

Eurodac's operational management shall cover all tasks necessary to ensure 24-hour operation, 7 days a week, in accordance with this Regulation, including the maintenance and technological developments necessary to ensure that the system functions satisfactorily. operational quality, in particular as regards the time required to request the central system. A business continuity plan and system should be developed, taking into account the need for maintenance and unforeseen interruptions in the operation of the system, including the impact of business continuity measures on data protection and security.

The Agency, in cooperation with the Member States, shall ensure that the best and most secure available technologies and techniques are always used for the Central System, provided that a cost-benefit analysis is carried out.

The Agency is responsible for the following tasks related to the communication infrastructure:

(a) supervision;

b) security;

(c) the coordination of relations between the Member States and the supplier.

The Commission shall be responsible for all tasks related to the Communication Infrastructure except those referred to in paragraph 2, in particular:

and • budget implementation;

b • acquisition and renewal;

• contractual issues.

The Agency shall apply appropriate rules of professional secrecy or other equivalent confidentiality obligations to all its staff who are required to handle Eurodac data. This obligation also applies after the employees leave their position or work or after the termination of their obligations.

Member State inspection bodies for law enforcement purposes

Each Member State shall designate a single national authority or body of that authority to act as its inspection body. The inspection body shall be the body of the Member State responsible for the prevention, detection or investigation of terrorist offenses or of other serious criminal offenses.

The notified body and the inspection body may be part of the same organization if national law so permits, but the inspection body shall act independently in carrying out the tasks assigned to it in accordance with this Regulation. The inspection body is separate from the operational units and does not receive instructions from them regarding the result of the inspection.

Member States may authorize more than one inspection body according to their organizational and administrative structures, in accordance with their constitutional and legal requirements.

The verifying authority shall satisfy itself that the conditions for requesting the comparison of fingerprints with Eurodac data are met.

Only duly authorized staff of the inspection body shall be entitled to receive and transmit a request for access to Eurodac.

Only the verifying authority is authorized to forward requests for comparison of fingerprints to the national access point.

Data storage

Each data set shall be stored in the Central System for a period of ten years from the date on which the fingerprints were taken.

After the expiration of the specified period, the Central System shall automatically delete this data from the Central System.

Pre-deletion of data

Data relating to a person who acquired the nationality of a Member State before the expiry of the period shall be deleted from the Central System as soon as the home Member State learns that the person concerned has acquired such nationality.

The Central System shall, as soon as possible and no later than 72 hours after the deletion, notify all home Member States of the deletion of data from another home Member State with which the data are Comparison of fingerprint data

In order to verify that a third-country national or a stateless person residing illegally in the territory of a Member State has not previously applied for international protection in another Member State, a Member State may submit to the Central System the fingerprint data on the fingerprints that may have been taken by such third-country national or stateless person who is at least 14 years old, as well as the reference number given by that Member State.

As a general rule, it should be checked whether a third-country national or a stateless person has not previously applied for international protection in another Member State where:

a • the third-country national or stateless person declares that he or she has applied for international protection, but does not indicate the Member State in which he or she applied;

b • the third-country national or stateless person has not applied for international protection but opposes being returned to his or her country of origin, claiming that he or she will be in danger there; or c • the third-country national or stateless person attempts to prevent his or her removal in another way by refusing to cooperate in establishing his or her identity, namely by not presenting any identity document or by presenting false identity documents.

Conditions for access to Eurodac by the designated authorities

For the purposes set out in the Regulation, the designated authorities may send a reasoned request in electronic form for the comparison of fingerprint data with those stored in the Central System, within the limits of the powers conferred on them, only if comparison with the following databases does not lead to the identity of the data subject:

- • national fingerprint databases;

- • the automated fingerprint identification systems of all other Member States under Decision 2008/615 / JHA, where the comparison is technically available, unless there are reasonable grounds for believing that the comparison with these systems will not lead to the identification of the the data subject. These valid reasons shall be included in the reasoned request in electronic form for comparison with the Eurodac data sent by the designated authority to the verifying authority; and

- • The Visa Information System, if the conditions for such comparison set out in Decision 2008/633 / JHA are met;

and when the following cumulative conditions are met:

and • the comparison is necessary for the purpose of preventing, detecting or investigating terrorist offenses or other serious criminal offenses, which means that there are very serious public security concerns which make searching the database proportionate;

b • the comparison is necessary in a certain case (ie no systematic comparisons will be made); and

c • there are reasonable grounds for believing that the comparison will significantly assist in the prevention, detection or investigation of any of the offenses in question. These valid reasons shall be present in particular where there is a reasonable suspicion that a suspected person, perpetrator or victim of a terrorist offense or other serious crime falls into a category covered by this Regulation.

Requests for comparison with Eurodac data are limited to searching for fingerprint data.

Conditions for access to Eurodac by Europol

For the purposes of the Regulation, the designated authority of Europol may send a reasoned request in electronic form for the comparison of fingerprint data with those stored in the Central System, within the competence of Europol and, where necessary, for the performance of Europol's tasks. , only if the comparison with fingerprint data stored in any data processing system that is technically and legally available to Europol does not lead to the identification of the data subject and when the following cumulative conditions are met:

a • and the comparison is necessary to support and strengthen Member States' actions to prevent, detect or investigate terrorist or other serious crimes covered by Europol's competence, which means that there is a very serious public security concern, which is why demand at the base data is proportional;

b • the comparison is necessary in a certain case (ie no systematic comparisons will be made); and

c • there are good reasons to believe that the comparison will significantly assist in the prevention, detection or investigation of any of the offenses in question. These valid reasons shall be present in particular where there is a reasonable suspicion that a suspected person, perpetrator or victim of a terrorist offense or other serious crime falls into a category covered by this Regulation.

Requests for comparison with Eurodac data are limited to comparing fingerprint data.

The home Member State must authorize the processing of information received from Europol as a result of a comparison with

Eurodac data. Such authorization shall be obtained through the national unit of Europol of that Member State.

Communication between designated authorities, inspection bodies and national access points

All communication between designated authorities, inspection bodies and national access points shall be secure and carried out electronically.

The fingerprints shall be digitally processed by the Member State and transmitted in the data format so that the comparison can be made by means of a computerized fingerprint recognition system.

Communication between Member States and the central system

The data transmitted by the Member States to the Central System and vice versa use the communication infrastructure. Where necessary, with a view to the proper functioning of the central system, the Agency shall lay down the technical procedures necessary for the use of the communication infrastructure.

Data security

The home Member State shall ensure the security of the data before and during transmission to the Central System.

Each Member State shall, in respect of all data processed by its competent authorities in accordance with this Regulation, take the necessary measures, including a security plan, to:

a • physical data protection, including through the preparation of contingency plans for critical infrastructure protection;

b • preventing unauthorized persons from gaining access to national installations where the Member State carries out operations in accordance with the objectives of Eurodac (checks at the entrance to the installation);

c • prevention of unauthorized reading, copying, modification or export of data carriers (control of data carriers);

d • prevention of unauthorized data entry and unauthorized verification, modification or deletion of stored personal data (storage control);

e • prevention of unauthorized processing of data in Eurodac and of any unauthorized change or deletion of data processed in Eurodac (control of data entry);

f • ensuring that persons entitled to access Eurodac have access only to the data to which they are granted access, through individual and unique usernames and only confidential access regimes (control of access to data);

(g) ensuring that all authorities with access to Eurodac create profiles describing the functions and responsibilities of the persons to whom access is granted and who have the right to enter, update, delete and search data, and whereas, at the request of the national supervisory authorities referred to in Article 28 of Directive 95/46 / EC and Article 25 of Framework Decision 2008/977 / JHA, they shall immediately provide them with those profiles (employee profiles) as well as any other relevant information, which the authorities may request for supervisory purposes;

h • ensuring the possibility to check and establish to which bodies personal data may be transferred through the use of communication equipment (communication control);

and • ensuring that it is possible to verify and establish which data have been processed in Eurodac, by whom and for what purpose (control of data registration);

• preventing the unauthorized reading, copying, modification or deletion of personal data during the transmission of personal data to or from Eurodac or during the transport of data carriers, in particular through appropriate encryption techniques (transport control);

• monitoring the effectiveness of security measures and taking the necessary organizational measures related to internal control to ensure compliance with this Regulation (own audit) and to automatically identify within 24 hours any relevant event arising from the implementation of measures that may indicate the occurrence of a security incident.

Member States shall notify the Agency of security incidents they have identified in their systems. The Agency shall notify the Member States, Europol and the European Data Protection Supervisor in the event of security incidents. The Member States concerned, the Agency and Europol shall cooperate in the event of a security incident.

Prohibition on the transfer of data to third countries or to international organizations or to private entities

Personal data received by a Member State or Europol under this Regulation from the Central System may not be transmitted or made available to a third country, an international organization or a private entity established inside or outside the Union. The prohibition shall also apply if such data are further processed at national level or between Member States within the meaning of Framework Decision 2008/977 / JHA.

Personal data originating from a Member State and exchanged between Member States as a result of a positive result shall not be transferred to third countries if there is a serious risk that, as a result of such transfer, the data subject may be subjected to inhuman or degrading treatment. and degrading treatment or punishment, or other violation of fundamental rights.

Registration and documentation

Each Member State and Europol shall ensure that all data processing operations resulting from requests for comparison with Eurodac data are recorded or documented for the purpose of verifying the admissibility of the request, the lawfulness of the data processing and the integrity and security of the data, as well as for the purposes of self-control.

The register or documentation shall in all cases contain the following elements:

a • the exact purpose of the request for comparison, including the type of terrorist or other serious crime in question, and for Europol, the exact purpose of the request for comparison;

b • the valid reasons for not comparing with other Member States in accordance with this Regulation;

c • the reference number of the national file;

d • the date and exact time of the request for comparison by the national central access unit;

e • the name of the authority that requested access for the purposes of the comparison and the responsible person who made the request and processed the data;

h • in accordance with national provisions or the provisions of Decision 2009/371 / JHA, the identification mark of the officer who carried out the search and of the officer who ordered the search or provision.

The registers and documentation are used only to control the lawfulness of the data processing, as well as to ensure the integrity and security of the data. The competent national supervisory authorities responsible for verifying the admissibility of the request and for verifying the lawfulness of the data processing and the integrity and security of the data shall be given access, on request, to those registers in order to be able to carry out their duties.

7.2. New large-scale information systems in the field of freedom, security and justice

7.2.1. European Travel Information and Authorization System (ETIAS)

ETIAS is an automated IT system designed to identify any security or illegal migration risks posed by visa-free visitors traveling to the Schengen area, while guaranteeing fundamental rights and data protection.

Third-country nationals who do not need a visa to travel to the Schengen area will have to apply for a travel authorization (ETIAS) before traveling.

After completing an online application form, the system will carry out checks on EU border and security information systems.

Preliminary verification of visa-free third-country nationals:

• facilitate border checks;

• will avoid bureaucracy and delays for passengers in presenting themselves at borders;

• ensure a coordinated and harmonized risk assessment of third-country nationals; and

• will significantly reduce the number of refusals to enter border crossings.

ETIAS stands for European Travel Information and Authorization System. This is an automated electronic system that monitors and allows entry into the Schengen area for visitors from countries whose citizens do not need a visa to enter the Schengen area. In a sense, this system is reminiscent of the US Electronic Entry Authorization (ESTA) system, which serves the same purpose. Work on the commissioning of the ETIAS system began in 2016 and the system is expected to be implemented by 2022.

Under ETIAS, each applicant will undergo a security check to determine whether he or she can be allowed to enter any Schengen country. As visitors from countries whose citizens do not need a visa for tourist purposes staying up to 90 days in the EU will not have to go through the long process of applying for a visa, the ETIAS system will have to make sure that these people do not represent security risk. This entry authorization system will collect, track and update the necessary information on visitors to determine whether their entry into the Schengen countries is safe.

In addition to using ETIAS for business and tourism purposes, the system will also allow you to visit Schengen countries for treatment and transit. In addition, it will be mandatory for all European countries for which a Schengen visa is not required.

In his 2016 Annual Communication, European Commission President Jean-Claude Juncker said:

"We need to know who is crossing our borders. So we will find out who is going to Europe before they come here. "

The main reason for applying for an ETIAS authorization is security. As the risks to travelers around the world increase, the EU wants to ensure safe entry into their countries. ETIAS will significantly reduce security concerns through the use of its information and data collection systems. This means that ETIAS will identify people who pose a threat to the security of the Schengen countries. This will lead to the fact that these people will be denied entry, which will avoid the threat of their presence in the EU. In fact, the system will solve the problem before it occurs.

Objectives of ETIAS

Assisting the competent authorities of the Member States, ETIAS shall:

and • contributes to a high level of security by providing for a thorough assessment of the security risk associated with applicants before arriving at external border crossing points to determine whether factual data are available or that there are reasonable grounds for the presence of a person in the territory of the Member States is considered to pose a security risk;

b • contributes to the prevention of illegal immigration by providing for an assessment of the risk of illegal immigration related to applicants before they arrive at external border crossing points;

c • contributes to the protection of public health by providing for an assessment of whether the applicant poses a high epidemic risk before arriving at external border crossing points;

d • increases the efficiency of border checks;

(e) help to achieve the objectives of the SIS in relation to alerts on third-country nationals who are refused entry and stay, alerts on wanted persons for the purpose of surrender or extradition, alerts on missing persons, alerts on persons who are wanted to assist in legal proceedings and alerts to persons for remote or explicit inspections;

f • contributes to the prevention, detection and investigation of terrorist or other serious crimes.

General structure of ETIAS

ETIAS consists of:
and • the ETIAS information system;
b • the ETIAS Central Unit;
in • ETIAS national units.

Construction and technical architecture of the ETIAS information system

1. The European Agency for the Operational Management of Large-Scale Information Systems in the Area of Freedom, Security and Justice ("eu-LISA") shall develop the ETIAS information system and ensure its technical management.

2. The ETIAS information system shall consist of:
and • a central ETIAS system, including the ETIAS watch list;

b • a national single interface (NUI) in each Member State, based on common technical specifications and the same for all Member States, allowing the secure connection of the ETIAS Central System to the national border infrastructures and to the central access points in the Member States;

c • communication infrastructure between the central ETIAS system and the national unified interfaces, which is protected and encrypted;

d • secure communication infrastructure between the ETIAS Central System and other information systems;

e • public website and mobile application;

is • e-mail service;

g • a secure account service that allows applicants to provide any additional information or required documentation;

h • a verification tool for applicants;

and • an instrument enabling applicants to provide or withdraw their consent for an additional period for keeping the application dossier;

j • a tool allowing Europol and the Member States to assess the potential impact on the share of manually processed applications as a result of inclusion in the ETIAS list for monitoring new data;

k • portal for carriers;

l • a secure web service allowing the ETIAS Central System to communicate with the public website, the mobile application, the e-mail service, the secure account service, the carrier portal, the applicant verification tool, the applicants' consent tool, the payment intermediary and Interpol databases;

m • software enabling the ETIAS Central Unit and the ETIAS National Units to process applications and consult with other ETIAS National Units;

n • central data warehouse for reporting and statistics purposes.

3. The central system of ETIAS, the national unified interfaces, web services, the carrier portal and the ETIAS communication infrastructure share and reuse as technically as possible the hardware and software components of the CIS central system, the CIS national

unified interfaces, the CIS web service and the CIS communication infrastructure.

ETIAS Central Unit

1. A central unit of ETIAS is hereby established in the European Border and Coast Guard Agency.

2. The ETIAS Central Unit shall operate 24 hours a day, 7 days a week. It replies:

a • in cases where the automated processing process has established compliance, to verify that the applicant's personal data match the personal data of the person who triggered that compliance, in the ETIAS Central System, including the ETIAS monitoring list, one of the information systems the EU reference, Europol data, any of the Interpol databases, or specific risk indicators indicated and, if a match is confirmed or if in doubt, to start the manual processing of the application;

b • to ensure that the data it enters in the application dossiers are up to date in accordance with the relevant provisions;

c • the identification, identification, ex-ante evaluation, implementation, ex-post evaluation, review and deletion of specific risk indicators after consultation of the ETIAS Board of Auditors;

d • to ensure that the checks and the corresponding results are recorded in the application dossiers;

e • to carry out regular audits of the processing of applications, including through regular assessments of their impact on fundamental rights, in particular with a view to respect for privacy and the protection of personal data;

f • to indicate, if necessary, the Member State responsible for the manual processing of applications;

(g) in the event of technical problems or unforeseen circumstances, to facilitate, if necessary, consultations between Member States as well as between the competent Member State and Europol;

h • to notify carriers in the event of a malfunction in the ETIAS information system;

and • to inform the ETIAS National Units of the Member States of a malfunction of the ETIAS information system;

j • for the processing of requests from Europol for reference to the data stored in the ETIAS Central System;

j • to provide the general public with all relevant information regarding the application for a travel authorization;

l • for the cooperation with the Commission regarding the information campaign;

m • to provide written support to travelers who have encountered problems completing the application form and have sought assistance through a standard contact form; to maintain an online list of frequently asked questions and answers;

n • to ensure follow-up and regular reporting to the Commission on reports of infringements by commercial intermediaries.

3. The ETIAS Central Unit shall publish an annual activity report. It includes statistics on:

and i • the number of travel authorizations issued automatically by the ETIAS Central System;

i • the number of applications checked by the ETIAS Central Unit;

• the number of applications processed manually by each Member State;

i • the number of applications refused by a third country and the reasons for the refusal;

v • the degree of compliance with the deadlines;

(b) general information on the functioning of the ETIAS Central Unit, its activities set out in this Article, and information on existing trends and challenges affecting the performance of its tasks.

The annual activity report shall be submitted to the European Parliament, the Council and the Commission by 31 March of the following year.

ETIAS National Units

1. Each Member State shall designate a competent authority as the national unit of ETIAS.

2. The national units of ETIAS shall be responsible for:

and • for the examination and decision-making of travel authorization applications, where the automated processing process has established compliance and where the ETIAS Central Unit has started manual processing of the application;

(b) to ensure that the tasks performed under point (a) and the corresponding results are recorded in the application dossiers;

c • to ensure that the data they enter in the application dossiers are up to date in accordance with the relevant provisions;

(d) to decide on the issue of a travel authorization with limited territorial validity as referred to in Article 44;

e • to ensure coordination with other national units of ETIAS and Europol in relation to requests for reference;

f • to provide information to applicants on the procedure to be followed in the event of an appeal;

g • for the revocation and revocation of a travel authorization.

3. Member States shall provide the national units of ETIAS with adequate resources to enable them to carry out their tasks in accordance with the time limits laid down in this Regulation.

Automated processing

1. Application dossiers shall be processed automatically by the ETIAS Central System to establish compliance.

The ETIAS Central System examines each application dossier separately.

2. The ETIAS Central System shall compare the relevant data with the data contained in a record, dossier or alert recorded in the ETIAS Central System, SIS, SVI, VIS, Eurodac, Europol data and the Interpol SLTD and TDAWN databases.

In particular, the ETIAS Central System shall verify:

and • whether the travel document used for the application corresponds to a travel document declared lost, stolen, misappropriated or invalid in the SIS;

b • whether the travel document used for the application corresponds to a travel document that has been declared lost, stolen or invalid in the SLTD;

c • whether an alert has been entered in the SIS for the applicant to refuse entry and stay;

(d) whether the applicant has an alert in the SIS relating to persons wanted for arrest for the purpose of surrender on the basis of a European arrest warrant or for the purpose of extradition;

e • whether the data on the applicant and the travel document correspond to the data on the refused, revoked or revoked travel authorization in the ETIAS Central System;

f • whether the data provided in the application regarding the travel document correspond to data in another application for a travel authorization in the ETIAS Central System related to different identity data;

g • whether the applicant is currently declared to have exceeded the permitted period of stay or has been declared as such in the past in the IAS;

h • whether it is recorded for the applicant that he has been denied entry into the SVI;

and • whether the applicant has been the subject of a VIS-registered decision to refuse, revoke or withdraw a short-stay visa;

j • whether the data provided in the application correspond to data recorded in Europol data;

j • whether the applicant is registered in Eurodac;

l • whether the travel document used for the application corresponds to a travel document registered in a TDAWN file;

m • if the applicant is a minor - whether for the person exercising parental rights over the applicant or who has been appointed as his legal guardian:

i • there is an alert in the SIS relating to persons wanted for arrest for the purpose of surrender on the basis of a European arrest warrant or for the purpose of extradition;

i • there is an entry in the SIS for denial of entry and stay.

ETIAS Inspection Board

1. An ETIAS Inspection Board shall be set up within the European Border and Coast Guard Agency to carry out advisory functions. It is composed of one representative from each ETIAS national unit, from the European Border and Coast Guard Agency and from Europol.

2. The ETIAS Board shall be consulted on inspections:

f • contributes to the prevention, detection and investigation of terrorist or other serious crimes.

General structure of ETIAS

ETIAS consists of:

and • the ETIAS information system;

b • the ETIAS Central Unit;

in • ETIAS national units.

Construction and technical architecture of the ETIAS information system

1. The European Agency for the Operational Management of Large-Scale Information Systems in the Area of Freedom, Security and Justice ("eu-LISA") shall develop the ETIAS information system and ensure its technical management.

2. The ETIAS information system shall consist of:

and • a central ETIAS system, including the ETIAS watch list;

b • a national single interface (NUI) in each Member State, based on common technical specifications and the same for all Member States, allowing the secure connection of the ETIAS Central System to the national border infrastructures and to the central access points in the Member States;

c • communication infrastructure between the central ETIAS system and the national unified interfaces, which is protected and encrypted;

d • secure communication infrastructure between the ETIAS Central System and other information systems;

e • public website and mobile application;

is • e-mail service;

g • a secure account service that allows applicants to provide any additional information or required documentation;

h • a verification tool for applicants;

and • an instrument enabling applicants to provide or withdraw their consent for an additional period for keeping the application dossier;

j • a tool allowing Europol and the Member States to assess the potential impact on the share of manually processed applications as a result of inclusion in the ETIAS list for monitoring new data;

k • portal for carriers;

l • a secure web service allowing the ETIAS Central System to communicate with the public website, the mobile application, the e-mail service, the secure account service, the carrier portal, the applicant verification tool, the applicants' consent tool, the payment intermediary and Interpol databases;

m • software enabling the ETIAS Central Unit and the ETIAS National Units to process applications and consult with other ETIAS National Units;

n • central data warehouse for reporting and statistics purposes.

4. The ETIAS Central System, the National Unified Interfaces, the Web Service, the Carrier Portal and the ETIAS Communication Infrastructure shall share and reuse as technically as possible the hardware and software components of the CIS Central System, the CIS National Unified Interfaces, the Web Service. of the SVI and of the communication infrastructure of the SVI.

ETIAS Central Unit

1. A central unit of ETIAS is hereby established in the European Border and Coast Guard Agency.

2. The ETIAS Central Unit shall operate 24 hours a day, 7 days a week. It replies:

a • in cases where an automated processing process has established compliance, to verify that the applicant's personal data match the personal data of the person who triggered that compliance, in the ETIAS Central System, including the ETIAS monitoring list, one of the information systems the EU reference, Europol data, any of the Interpol databases, or specific risk indicators indicated and, if a match is confirmed or if in doubt, to start the manual processing of the application;

b • to ensure that the data it enters in the application dossiers are up to date in accordance with the relevant provisions;

c • the identification, identification, ex-ante evaluation, implementation, ex-post evaluation, review and deletion of specific risk indicators after consultation of the ETIAS Board of Auditors;

d • to ensure that the checks and the corresponding results are recorded in the application dossiers;

e • to carry out regular audits of the processing of applications, including through regular assessments of their impact on fundamental rights, in particular with a view to respect for privacy and the protection of personal data;

f • to indicate, if necessary, the Member State responsible for the manual processing of applications;

(g) in the event of technical problems or unforeseen circumstances, to facilitate, if necessary, consultations between Member States as well as between the competent Member State and Europol;

h • to notify carriers in the event of a malfunction in the ETIAS information system;

and • to inform the ETIAS National Units of the Member States of a malfunction of the ETIAS information system;

j • for the processing of requests from Europol for reference to the data stored in the central office of the ETIAS;

j • to provide the general public with all relevant information in relation to the application for a travel authorization;

l • for the cooperation with the Commission regarding the information campaign;

m • to provide written support to travelers who have encountered problems completing the application form and have sought assistance through a standard contact form; to maintain an online list of frequently asked questions and answers;

n • to ensure follow-up and regular reporting to the Commission on reports of infringements by commercial intermediaries.

3. The ETIAS Central Unit shall publish an annual activity report. It includes statistics on:

and i • the number of travel authorizations issued automatically by the ETIAS Central System;

i • the number of applications checked by the ETIAS Central Unit;

• the number of applications processed manually by each Member State;

i • the number of applications refused by a third country and the reasons for the refusal;

v • the degree of compliance with the deadlines;

(b) general information on the functioning of the ETIAS Central Unit, its activities set out in this Article, and information on existing trends and challenges affecting the performance of its tasks.

The annual activity report shall be submitted to the European Parliament, the Council and the Commission by 31 March of the following year.

ETIAS National Units

1. Each Member State shall designate a competent authority as the national unit of ETIAS.

2. The national units of ETIAS shall be responsible for:

and • for the examination and decision-making of travel authorization applications, where the automated processing process has established compliance and where the ETIAS Central Unit has started manual processing of the application;

(b) to ensure that the tasks performed under point (a) and the corresponding results are recorded in the application dossiers;

c • to ensure that the data they enter in the application dossiers are up to date in accordance with the relevant provisions;

(d) to decide on the issue of a travel authorization with limited territorial validity as referred to in Article 44;

e • to ensure coordination with other national units of ETIAS and Europol in relation to requests for reference;

f • to provide information to applicants on the procedure to be followed in the event of an appeal;

g • for the revocation and revocation of a travel authorization.

3. Member States shall provide the national units of ETIAS with adequate resources to enable them to carry out their tasks in accordance with the time limits laid down in this Regulation.

Automated processing

1. Application dossiers shall be processed automatically by the ETIAS Central System to establish compliance. The ETIAS Central System examines each application dossier separately.

2. The ETIAS Central System shall compare the relevant data with the data contained in a record, dossier or alert recorded in the ETIAS Central System, SIS, SVI, VIS, Eurodac, Europol data and the Interpol SLTD and TDAWN databases.

In particular, the ETIAS Central System shall verify:

and • whether the travel document used for the application corresponds to a travel document declared lost, stolen, misappropriated or invalid in the SIS;

b • whether the travel document used for the application corresponds to a travel document that has been declared lost, stolen or invalid in the SLTD;

c • whether an alert has been entered in the SIS for the applicant to refuse entry and stay;

(d) whether the applicant has an alert in the SIS relating to persons wanted for arrest for the purpose of surrender on the basis of a European arrest warrant or for the purpose of extradition;

e • whether the data on the applicant and the travel document correspond to the data on the refused, revoked or revoked travel authorization in the ETIAS Central System;

f • whether the data provided in the application regarding the travel document correspond to data in another application for a travel authorization in the ETIAS Central System related to different identity data;

g • whether the applicant is currently declared to have exceeded the permitted period of stay or has been declared as such in the past in the IAS;

h • whether it is recorded for the applicant that he has been denied entry into the SVI;

and • whether the applicant has been the subject of a VIS-registered decision to refuse, revoke or withdraw a short-stay visa;

j • whether the data provided in the application correspond to data recorded in Europol data;

j • whether the applicant is registered in Eurodac;

l • whether the travel document used for the application corresponds to a travel document registered in a TDAWN file;

m • if the applicant is a minor - whether for the person exercising parental rights over the applicant or who has been appointed as his legal guardian:

i • there is an alert in the SIS relating to persons wanted for arrest for the purpose of surrender on the basis of a European arrest warrant or for the purpose of extradition;

i • there is an entry in the SIS for denial of entry and stay.

ETIAS Inspection Board

1. An ETIAS Inspection Board shall be set up within the European Border and Coast Guard Agency to carry out advisory functions. It is composed of one representative from each ETIAS national unit, from the European Border and Coast Guard Agency and from Europol.

2. The ETIAS Board shall be consulted on inspections:

a • by the ETIAS Central Unit on the identification, identification, ex ante evaluation, implementation, ex-post evaluation, review and deletion of specific risk indicators;

b • by Member States on the implementation of the ETIAS watch list;

c • by Europol on the implementation of the ETIAS watch list.

3. The ETIAS Inspection Board shall draw up opinions, guidelines, recommendations and good practices for the purposes referred to in paragraph 2. When making recommendations, the ETIAS Inspection Board shall take into account the recommendations issued by the ETIAS Fundamental Rights Guidelines.

4. The ETIAS Inspection Board shall meet as necessary, but not less than twice a year. The costs and support of its meetings shall be borne by the European Border and Coast Guard Agency.

5. On specific issues relating to fundamental rights, in particular with regard to respect for privacy, personal data protection and non-discrimination, the ETIAS Inspection Board may consult the ETIAS Board for guidance on fundamental rights.

6. At its first meeting, the ETIAS Inspection Board shall adopt its rules of procedure by a simple majority of its members.

Interoperability with other EU information systems

1. Interoperability shall be established between the ETIAS information system, other EU information systems and Europol data in order to facilitate the verification referred to in Article 20.

2. Amendments to the legal acts establishing the EU information systems necessary to ensure their interoperability with ETIAS, as well

as the addition of the relevant provisions to this Regulation, shall be the subject of a separate legal instrument.

Search Interpol databases

The ETIAS Central System searches the Interpol Database for Stolen or Missing Travel Documents (SLTD) and the Interpol Database for Travel Documents Related to Newsletters (TDAWN). All inquiries and inspections shall be carried out in such a way that no information is disclosed on the object of the Interpol signal.

Overall, the ETIAS authorization will make travel to the EU less problematic and much safer.

The ETIAS authorization is not a visa. Once operational, the system will carry out pre-journey checks on passengers who can travel to the Schengen area without a visa, in order to identify migration and security risks. Upon arrival at the EU borders, travelers will need to have both a valid travel document and an ETIAS permit.

Completing an online application should not take more than 10 minutes, and in over 95% of cases automatic approval is obtained. Travelers will have to pay a one-time fee of 7 euros (for passengers between the ages of 18 and 70), and the permit will be valid for three years.

ETIAS will cross-check the data provided with visa-exempt passengers in the information systems of the The EU in the field of borders, security and migration, including the Schengen Information System (SIS), the Visa Information System (VIS), Eurodac and the Europol and Interpol databases. If cross-checking of the data leads to the detection of compliance with data contained in EU databases, the application will be examined manually by the ETIAS Central Unit, managed by the European Border and Coast Guard Agency.

Thanks to its modernization, eu-LISA - the EU's agency for the operational management of large-scale information systems in the area of freedom, security and justice - will have the capacity and tools it needs to ensure centralized operational management of EU in the field of migration, security and border management.

The Agency will also be in a better position to maintain and modernize existing systems, such as the Schengen Information System (SIS), the Visa Information System (VIS) and Eurodac, for which it is already responsible. The reinforced agency will be responsible for implementing technical solutions to ensure that these EU information systems interact effectively and are easily accessible to local police and border guards.

7.2.2. EU entry / exit system (EES)

In 2015, more than 50 million non-EU citizens visited the European Union, representing more than 200 million border crossings. The growth of cross-border travel is expected to continue, as the number of non-EU travelers is estimated to increase to 76 million by 2025. At the same time, the unprecedented migration flow to the EU peaked in 2015, with 1.8 million irregular border crossings reported by Frontex. In 2016, there was a decrease, but more than half a million irregular border crossings were still opened, which is higher than any annual figure for arrivals between 2010 (104,060) and 2014 (282,933). Border management capacity has been exhausted at the main points of irregular entry at the EU's external border, allowing mixed flows of asylum seekers and migrants to move further within the EU Schengen area. These developments are putting strong pressure on the Schengen area of free movement, which is seen as one of the EU's most recognizable achievements and creates tensions between Member States.

Moreover, increased passenger flows must be seen in a new security context, not least because of the risks of serious crime and terrorism stemming from the threat posed by ISIL / Da'esh, radicalization and foreign fighters.

Following the terrorist attacks in Europe in 2015, 2016 and 2017, a number of gaps in the use of information exchange tools between Member States have been identified.

In anticipation of increased passenger flows and in response to security concerns regarding the control of the EU's external borders, on 6 April 2016, the Commission presented a revised proposal to set up an entry / exit system to register all non-citizens at border crossings. EU They are based on the Smart Borders package presented in 2013, which did not provide consensus among co-legislators and was the subject of further technical and operational studies completed in 2015.

The current system for manual stamping of passports will be replaced by automation of some preparatory procedures for border control. The system will be connected to the Visa Information System

(VIS) database and will be used by the same authorities: border checkpoints and consulates. This would allow law enforcement to execute limited queries in the criminal identification and intelligence database to prevent serious crime and terrorism. Both regulations were signed on November 30, 2017, and the entry / exit system should become fully operational by 2020 at the latest.

Current status

In the field of border management, the EU has developed three centralized information systems, which have different objectives: the Schengen Information System (SIS); Visa Information System (VIS); and Eurodac. While VIS and Eurodac focus on third-country nationals and have law enforcement as an aid objective, the SIS is also important for EU citizens and directly supports both external border control and law enforcement cooperation.

In addition to the three central systems developed by the EU, a number of other information systems related to border management and / or law enforcement are available in the EU, each with a specific institution, legal and political context. Examples are the database of stolen and lost travel documents of Interpol, advance Information for passengers (passenger information before incoming flights to the EU) and the European Criminal Records Information System (ECRIS).

While existing border control and / or law enforcement cooperation information systems cover a wide range of data and functionalities, this complex landscape includes some shortcomings: different management systems; information gaps; fragmentation; limited interoperability and possible database mismatch.

An information gap identified by the European Commission concerns the systematic registration of movements for crossing external borders of all third-country nationals visiting the Schengen area for a short stay (maximum 90-day period for each period of 180 days) and the related tracking the time spent inside the area. Currently, the only means by which the relevant authorities have to calculate the length of stay of a third-country national in the Schengen area and to check their potential stay is a travel document stamped by them with the dates of entry and exit. This method is considered slow and error prone, as entry / exit stamps can be illegible or false.

According to the Commission, this information gap could have a negative impact on a number of areas, including: the quality and speed of border controls involving third-country nationals; systematic and reliable monitoring of the permitted stay of third-country nationals in the Schengen area; and the ability to identify third-country nationals who have destroyed their official documents after entering the Schengen area. With a view to removal In the light of these shortcomings, the European Commission has put forward a revised proposal to set up an entry / exit system (EES), a new centralized information system based on biometric data that would be interconnected with the VIS and targeted at third-country nationals.

Comparative elements

In February 2013, the Commission announced that 13 EU Member States (Bulgaria, Cyprus, Estonia, Finland, Hungary, Latvia, Lithuania, Malta, Poland, Portugal, Romania, Slovakia and Spain) have national entry / exit, collection systems. of the relevant records of third-country nationals crossing the external borders of the countries concerned. However, these systems cannot provide data on the flow and movement of third-country nationals across the external borders of the Schengen area, as they are not linked to similar systems in other Member States. For example, a third-country national entering the zone in a Member State may use such a national system to leave another Member State, which makes it impossible for entry and exit records to match.

Preparation of the proposal

The first version of the Smart Borders package, presented in 2013, raised a number of controversial issues which were subsequently assessed in the so-called "proof of concept" exercise to assess the technical, organizational and financial impact of possible solutions. The first phase of the exercise consisted of an additional technical study (including a new cost analysis), completed in October 2014, which examined a number of options related to biometrics, border control processes, data, architecture and costs, with a view to identifying a limited number of suitable solutions to be tested in the next phase. The second phase, a one-year pilot project carried out by the European Agency for the Operational Management of Large-Scale IT Systems (eu-LISA), tested the identified set of technical options against measurable criteria (eg accuracy, efficiency and impact on border crossing time), added results with desk research and collected feedback from passengers and border guards. In November 2015, the final report of the pilot project positively assessed the possibility of using biometric identifiers at the external Schengen borders. Evidence of a conceptual exercise and consideration of a number of important developments that have intervened since the presentation of the initial proposal (eg visa liberalization dialogues; Court of Justice) on the Data Retention Directive; and a political agreement between the EP and the Council on data protection reform), contributed to the revision of the 2013 package. This led to a revised EES proposal and the withdrawal of the proposal to establish a centralized registered passenger program (RTP). The most revised proposal is accompanied by a new impact assessment.

According to the multiannual financial framework for the period 2014-2020, the financial implications of the EES proposal are covered by the Border and Visa Facility of the Internal Security Fund (ISF), which allocates EUR 791 million for the development of IT systems to support the management of migration flows. across the EU outside borders. The revised EES proposal estimates the necessary budget for the new system at EUR 480 million, which will allow the remaining

EUR 311 million to be reallocated to other ISF measures, as set out in Regulation (EU) № 515/2014 The financial resources the Commission deems necessary were reduced by € 1.1 billion in 2008.

2013, when the figures covered two systems (EES and RTP) instead of EES alone, and a longer period of time (development and operation between 2015 and 2020 compared to 2017-2020 in the new proposal).

In addition, the changes included in the new EES proposal have had an impact on the estimated costs of the system - for example, to consider the technical possibilities for interoperability with other systems, as well as the higher costs associated with a longer data retention period. .

According to the Commission, the design of the proposal draws lessons from previous developments in other large-scale IT systems, such as the second generation Schengen Information System (SIS II), to which the European Court of Auditors has dedicated its special report 3/2014. In particular, the Commission says that the proposal: 1) makes development conditional on final adoption by the main legal instruments in order to avoid cost overruns and delays due to changing system requirements; 2) include in the budget of EUR 480 million the reimbursement of all integration costs incurred by the Member States in order to avoid possible delays in the development of the system at national level and to enable the Commission to monitor the progress of these developments; and 3) eu-LISA tasks with the development of not only a central system but also a common national single interface (NUI) to facilitate the coordination of implementation.

The changes that the proposal would make

The proposal outlines three main objectives: 1) improving the management of the external borders; 2) reduction of illegal migration; and 3) to contribute to the fight against terrorism and serious forms of organized crime and to ensure a high level of internal security.

One of the main changes will be the manual stamping of passports at border checks replaced by registration in a database. The proposal allows Member States to automate most of the steps taken to capture data and information currently taken by border guards at border checks of non-EU citizens. The new system will apply to all TCNs, whether required or visa-free, thus significantly expanding the EU's biometric information system. To balance the expansion, the biometric dataset will be reduced compared to the previous proposal (four fingerprints and face images instead of 10 fingerprints).

Using self-service systems and electronic ports, TCN passengers would check their data, their picture or fingerprint and a set of questions. Visa applicants will also be able to see the maximum length of their stay. While using the self-service system, all mandatory checks will be triggered in the security databases (database for stolen and lost travel documents for SIS, Interpol). At the time the passenger is directed to the border control strip, all this information would reach the border guard, who can ask additional questions before giving passengers access to the Schengen area. The power system will be used by the same authorities as already use VIS: consular posts and border control. The EES and the VIS can be interconnected, which would help to reduce duplication of data processing, in accordance with the principle of "design confidentiality". The Commission states that the EES would fit within the current management architecture and be interoperable with existing systems.

Automating the preparatory steps is expected to reduce the workload of border guards. This would mean that Member States would not have to hire additional border guards to accommodate the growing passenger flows. Long queues are also expected to be reduced before passengers reach the border crossing. The most

The Commission notes that the automated preparation phase would free up border guards' time, which could be used more valuable to assess each situation, thus contributing to enhanced internal security.

In the same vein, another important change is the access of law enforcement authorities to the EES, allowing national law enforcement authorities as well as Europol to make inquiries about crime detection and criminal intelligence. As expected results, the Commission claims that the EES will support the identification of terrorists, criminals and suspects, but also victims of crime. By providing a record of their travel history, it would complement the alerts recorded in the SIS

The IAS will be an automated information system for registering the entry and exit of passengers, citizens of non-EU countries, across the external borders. It will be used both for citizens who need a short-stay visa and for third-country nationals who are exempt from the visa requirement.

The IAS will replace the current system of manual stamping of passports, which takes time, does not provide reliable data on border crossings and does not allow the effective detection of persons who have exceeded their stay. The system will also contribute to the fight against terrorism and serious crime.

Subject

Regulation (EU) 2017/2226 establishes an IAS, a common electronic system that:

• records and stores the date, time and place of entry and exit of citizens of non-EU countries crossing EU borders;

• automatically calculates the length of stay of such third-country nationals and alerts EU countries when the length of stay has expired.

The system replaces the requirement to stamp the passports of third-country nationals, which is applied by all EU countries.

Purpose:

• to assist in the modernization of the management of the external borders by improving the quality and effectiveness of checks at the external borders of the Schengen area,

• to strengthen internal security and the fight against terrorism and serious crime,

• to help Member States deal with the ever-increasing number of people traveling to the EU, without having to increase the number of border guards,

• to systematically identify the persons who have exceeded the permitted period of stay (persons residing in the Schengen area after the end of their permitted stay).

Scope

The IAS applies to passengers who are required to have a visa, as well as to those exempted from this requirement and admitted for a short stay of up to 90 days within a 180-day period crossing the external borders of the Schengen area. The IAS will also record information on third-country nationals who have been refused entry for a short stay.

The IAS will operate at the external borders of the EU countries that are fully implementing the Schengen acquis and at the borders of the EU countries which, at the time of the start of the system, will not yet fully apply the Schengen acquis. , but will have successfully passed the Schengen evaluation procedure and received passive access to the VIS and full access to the Schengen Information System (SIS).

Data storage and accessibility

SVI will store identity data, travel documents, and biometric data. The data will be stored for 3 years for those passengers who comply with the rules for short stays and 5 years for those who exceed the permitted period of stay.

The retained data will be available to border authorities, visa authorities and authorities responsible for monitoring whether a third-country national fulfills the conditions of entry or residence. For the purposes of prevention, detection or the investigation of terrorist offenses or other serious criminal offenses, the relevant law enforcement authorities and Europol may request consultation with CIS data.

Technical architecture

SVI consists of:

• a central system that manages a computerized central database with biometric and alphanumeric data (a mixture of letters and numbers);

• a national single interface in each participating country;

• a secure channel of communication between the central IMS system and the central VIS;

• secure and encrypted communication infrastructure between the central system of the CIS and the national unified interfaces (identical interfaces for all EU countries connect their border infrastructures to the central system of the CIS);

• data warehouse for receiving personalized reports and statistics;

• a web service to allow third-country nationals to check their remaining authorized stay.

Eu-LISA is responsible for the development and management of the system, including the adaptation of the VIS to ensure interoperability between the Central IMS and the Central VIS.

Amendment of the Schengen Borders Code

Regulation (EU) 2017/2225 amends the Schengen Borders Code regarding the use of CIS at the EU's external borders. These changes include the following:

• the entry and exit of third-country nationals is recorded directly in the IAS;

• where explicitly provided for in its national legislation, an EU country may continue to stamp the travel documents of third-country nationals if they hold a residence permit or a long-stay visa issued by that EU country;

• third-country nationals must provide biometric data for the creation of their personal file in the IAS or for carrying out border checks;

• the identity, nationality, authenticity and validity of the travel document of third-country nationals for crossing the border are verified;

• EU countries can draw up national programs to facilitate the entry on a voluntary basis for ex-ante third-country nationals;

• EU countries can decide whether and to what extent to use technologies such as self-service systems for third-country nationals for pre-recording or updating data in CIS, e-portals and automated border control systems, provided that appropriate the degree of certainty that their use is monitored and that border guards have access to the results of these border checks.

Expected results from the Entry / Exit System

It will provide: - accurate information provided in a rapid and automatic manner to border guards during border checks, - information provided to border guards on refusals of entry for non-EU nationals and the possibility for entry refusals to be checked electronically in the Entry / Exit System, - accurate information for passengers on the maximum length of their stay, - accurate information on persons who have exceeded their authorized time on the basis of facts, assistance in the development of visa policy. With regard to access for law enforcement purposes, the Entry / Exit System is expected to: - assist in the identification of terrorists, criminals, as well as suspects and victims of crime, - provide data on past trips of citizens of countries outside The EU, including suspects and perpetrators or victims of crime. In this way, it complements the information in the SIS.

Assessing the use of intelligent surveillance technologies in border control, commentators pointed out that the EES's goal of catching excess visas is not entirely viable, as it will only identify people crossing external borders and not those who stay in the EU irregularly. Regarding the obligation to provide personal and biometric information when crossing the border, they comply with this refusal to fingerprint or if you have an image of the person, this may lead to viewing the passenger as a risk.

7.2.3. Centralized system for establishing Member States with information on convictions against third-country nationals and stateless persons (ECRIS-TCN)

ECRIS-TCN technical structure

ECRIS-TCN consists of:

a • a central system in which information on the identity of convicted third-country nationals is stored;

b • a national central access point in each Member State;

c • interface software enabling the competent authorities to connect to the central system through the national central access point and the communication infrastructure referred to in point (d);

d • communication infrastructure between the central system and the national central access points.

Data entry in ECRIS-TCN

For each convicted third-country national, the central authority of the convicting Member State shall create a data record in the Central System. The data record contains:

and for alphanumeric data:

i • information to be included, unless in some cases this information is known to the central authority (mandatory information):

- surname,
- proper names,
- date of birth,
- place of birth (city and country),
- citizenship of one or more countries,
- sex,
- previous names, if applicable,
- the code of the convicting Member State,

(ii) information to be included if entered in criminal records (optional information):

- names of the parents;

(iii) information to be included if available to the Central Authority (additional information):

- identification number or type and number of the identity documents of the person, as well as the name of the issuing body;

- aliases or other names used.

(b) on fingerprint data:

i • data on fingerprints that have been taken in accordance with national law in criminal proceedings;

i • at least, fingerprint data based on one of the following criteria:

• when the third-country national has received a sentence of imprisonment of at least 6 months;

or

• where the third-country national has been convicted of an offense punishable under the law of a Member State by a maximum term of imprisonment of at least 12 months;

The recording of data may also include portraits of the convicted third-country national, if the law of the convicting Member State in which the sentence was handed down allows the collection and storage of portraits of convicted persons.

The convicting Member State shall create the data record in an automated manner where possible and without undue delay after the sentence has been entered in the criminal records.

Portrait photos

Pending the entry into force of the delegated act, portraits may only be used to confirm the identity of a third-country national established as a result of a search of alphanumeric data or a search of fingerprint data.

The Commission shall be empowered to adopt delegated acts to supplement this Regulation on the use of portraits for the purpose of establishing the identity of third-country nationals, in order to identify Member States with information on previous convictions of such persons, where applicable. technically possible. Before exercising this power, the Commission shall, taking into account the necessity and proportionality as well as technological innovations in the field of facial recognition software, assess the availability and availability of the technology concerned.

Use of ECRIS-TCN to identify Member States with information from criminal records

Central authorities shall use ECRIS-TCN to identify Member States that have information from criminal records for a third-country national in order to obtain information on previous convictions through ECRIS, where information from criminal records for that person is required in the Member State concerned. for the purposes of criminal proceedings against that person or for any other of the above the following objectives, if provided for under national law and in accordance with it:
- • checking the person's own criminal record at his request,
- access permits,
- • obtaining a license or permit,
- • a reliability study for the purpose of employment,
- • a study on the reliability of voluntary activities, which include direct and regular contact with children or vulnerable persons,
- • visa issuance, citizenship and migration-related procedures, including asylum procedures, and
- • inspections in connection with public procurement contracts and open tenders.

However, in individual cases other than those in which a third-country national requests information from the central authority about his or her own criminal record or where the request is made in order to obtain information from criminal records in accordance with Article 10 (2) of Directive 2011/93 / EU, the authority requesting information from criminal records may decide that the use of ECRIS-TCN is not appropriate.

Eurojust, Europol and the European Public Prosecutor's Office may carry out an inspection in ECRIS-TCN in order to identify Member States that have information from criminal records for a third-country national. However, they do not enter, correct or delete data in ECRIS-TCN.

The competent authorities may also carry out a check in ECRIS-TCN to verify that there is a Member State with a Member State that has information from the criminal record for the same person as a third-country national.

In the case of open compliance, the Central System shall automatically provide the competent authority with information on the Member States having information from the criminal records of the third-country national concerned, together with the relevant reference numbers and relevant identity information. This identity information shall be used only for the purpose of verifying the identity of the third-country national concerned.

In the absence of compliance, the Central System shall automatically inform the competent authority.

Data retention period

Each data record shall be stored in the Central System for as long as the data on the convictions against the person concerned are kept in the criminal records.

Upon expiry of the storage period, the Central Authority of the sentencing Member State shall delete from the Central System the recording of data, including data on fingerprints or portraits. Deletion shall be carried out in an automated manner whenever possible and in any case not later than one month after the expiry of the storage period.

Modifying and deleting data

Member States may amend or delete the data they have entered in ECRIS-TCN.

Any alteration of the information in the criminal records which resulted in the creation of a data record in accordance with Article 5 shall include an identical modification of the information stored in that data record in the Central System by the convicting Member State without undue delay.

If a convicting Member State has reason to believe that data recorded in the Central System are inaccurate or have been processed in the Central System in breach of this Regulation, it shall:

a • immediately initiate a procedure to verify the accuracy of the data concerned or the lawfulness of their processing, if appropriate;

b • if necessary, without undue delay, correct the data or delete them from the central system.

If a Member State other than the convicting Member State which entered the data has reason to believe that the data recorded in the Central System are inaccurate or have been processed in the Central System in breach of this Regulation, it shall contact the Central Authority without undue delay. of the convicting Member State.

The convicting Member State:

a • immediately initiate a procedure to verify the accuracy of the data concerned or the lawfulness of their processing, if appropriate;

b • if necessary, without undue delay, correct the data or delete them from the central system;

c • notifies the other Member State without undue delay of the correction or deletion of the data or of the reasons why the data have not been corrected or deleted.

Development and operational management of ECRIS-TCN

eu-LISA is responsible for the development of ECRIS-TCN in accordance with the principle of data protection during design and default. In addition, eu-LISA is responsible for the operational management of ECRIS-TCN. The development consists in the preparation and implementation of technical specifications, testing and overall project coordination.

eu-LISA is also responsible for further developing and maintaining the ECRIS connectivity application template.

eu-LISA designs the physical structure of ECRIS-TCN, including its technical specifications and developments with respect to the Central System, the National Central Access Point and the interface software. This draft shall be adopted by the eu-LISA Management Board subject to a favorable opinion from the Commission.

eu-LISA shall develop and implement ECRIS-TCN as soon as possible after the entry into force of this Regulation and after the Commission has adopted the implementing acts provided for in Article 10.

Prior to the design and development phase of ECRIS-TCN, the eu-LISA Governing Board shall set up a ten-member Program Management Board.

The Program Management Board shall consist of eight members appointed by the Governing Board, the Chair of the ECRIS-TCN Advisory Group and one member appointed by the Commission. The members appointed by the Governing Board shall be elected only by those Member States which, under Union law, are fully bound by the legislative instruments governing ECRIS and which participate in ECRIS-TCN. The Governing Board shall ensure that the members it appoints to the Program Management Board have the necessary experience and knowledge in the development and management of information systems to support the judiciary and the authorities responsible for criminal records.

eu-LISA participates in the work of the Program Management Board. To this end, eu-LISA representatives shall attend the meetings of the Program Management Board to report on the design and development work of ECRIS-TCN and other related activities.

The Program Management Board shall meet at least once every three months, and more frequently if necessary. It ensures proper management of the ECRIS-TCN design and development phase and ensures coherence between the central and national ECRIS-TCN projects and the national ECRIS connectivity software. The Program Management Board shall submit to the eu-LISA Management Board regularly and, if possible, monthly written reports on the progress of the project. The Program Management Board does not have decision-making powers or a mandate to represent the members of the Management Board.

The Program Management Board shall adopt its rules of procedure, which shall include in particular rules on:

a • the presidency;

b • the venues of the meetings;

c • preparation of meetings;

d • the participation of experts in the meetings;

e • communication plans to ensure full information of non-participating board members.

The Program Management Board shall be chaired by a Member State which, under Union law, is fully bound by the legislative instruments governing ECRIS and the legislative instruments governing the development, creation, operation and use of all large-scale information systems managed by eu-LISA. .

To ensure the confidentiality and integrity of the data stored in ECRIS-TCN at all times, eu-LISA shall, in cooperation with the Member States, provide appropriate technical and organizational measures, taking into account the state of the art, implementation costs and risks associated with processing.

eu-LISA is responsible for the following tasks related to the communication infrastructure):

a • supervision;

b • security;

c • coordinating relations between Member States and the communication infrastructure provider.

The Commission shall be responsible for all other tasks related to the communication infrastructure referred to in Article 4 (1) (d), in particular:

and • budget implementation tasks;

b • acquisition and renewal;

in • contractual matters.

eu-LISA develops and maintains a mechanism and procedures for carrying out quality checks on data stored in ECRIS-TCN and submits regular reports to Member States. eu-LISA submits regular reports to the Commission covering the problems encountered and the Member States concerned.

The operational management of ECRIS-TCN shall cover all tasks necessary to ensure the proper functioning of ECRIS-TCN in accordance with this Regulation, and in particular the maintenance and technical development necessary to ensure that ECRIS-TCN operates with satisfactory quality in compliance with technical specifications.

eu-LISA performs tasks related to the provision of training on the technical use of ECRIS-TCN and the model ECRIS connection application.

Responsibilities of the Member States

Each Member State shall be responsible for:

a • ensuring a secure connection between its national criminal records and fingerprint databases and the national central access point;

b • the development, operation and maintenance of the connection;

c • providing a link between its national system and the ECRIS connection model;

Before authorizing them to process data stored in the Central System, each Member State shall provide appropriate training to the staff members of its Central Authority who have the right to access ECRIS-TCN, covering in particular the rules on data security and protection and applicable fundamental rights.

Responsibility for the use of data

In accordance with the applicable Union data protection rules, each Member State shall ensure that the data recorded in ECRIS-TCN are processed lawfully, in particular that:

a • only duly authorized staff have access to them to carry out their tasks;

b • the data are collected lawfully and in full respect of the human dignity and fundamental rights of the third-country national;

c • the data are legally entered in ECRIS-TCN;

d • the data is accurate and up-to-date when entered into ECRIS-TCN.

Access to Eurojust, Europol and the European Public Prosecutor's Office

Eurojust shall have direct access to ECRIS-TCN for the application of Article 17, as well as for the performance of the tasks provided for in Article 2 of Regulation (EU) 2018/1727, in order to identify Member States with information on previous convictions of citizens. of third countries.

Europol has direct access to ECRIS-TCN in order to identify Member States with information on previous convictions of third-country nationals.

The European Public Prosecutor's Office has direct access to ECRIS-TCN to carry out its tasks in order to identify Member States with information on previous convictions of third-country nationals.

Once a match has been found indicating Member States with information from criminal records concerning a third-country national, Eurojust, Europol and the European Public Prosecutor's Office may use their respective contacts with the national authorities of those Member States to request information from the registries. criminal record in the manner provided for in their respective constituent acts.

Access by authorized officials of Eurojust, Europol and the European Public Prosecutor's Office

Eurojust, Europol and the European Public Prosecutor's Office shall be responsible for managing the access and access measures of duly authorized staff to ECRIS-TCN in accordance with this Regulation and for establishing and regularly updating a list of those staff and their profiles.

Responsibilities of Eurojust, Europol and the European Public Prosecutor's Office

Eurojust, Europol and the European Public Prosecutor's Office:

a • determine the technical means for connection to ECRIS-TCN and are responsible for maintaining this connection;

(b) provide appropriate training, covering in particular data security and data protection rules, as well as the applicable fundamental rights for those staff members who have the right to access ECRIS-TCN before authorizing them to process data stored in the central system .;

(c) ensure that personal data which they process under this Regulation are protected in accordance with the applicable data protection rules.

Contact point for third countries and international organizations

Third countries and international organizations may, for the purposes of criminal proceedings, request Eurojust information on Member States, if any, which hold information from criminal records for third-country nationals. To that end, they shall use the standard form set out in the Annex to this Regulation.

When Eurojust receives a request under paragraph 1, the Agency shall use ECRIS-TCN to determine which Member States, if any, have information from the criminal records for the third-country national concerned.

If there is compliance, Eurojust shall ask the Member State which has information from the criminal records of the third-country national concerned whether it agrees to inform Eurojust of the third country or international organization of the name of the Member State concerned. If that Member State gives its consent, Eurojust shall inform the third country or international organization of the name of that Member State and how a request for an extract from the criminal record in that Member State may be made in accordance with the applicable procedures.

Where no compliance is found or where Eurojust is unable to respond in accordance with paragraph 3 to requests made pursuant to this Article, it shall inform the third country or international organization concerned that it has completed the procedure, without indicating whether any Member State has with information from the criminal records for the person concerned.

CONCLUSION

The firm and unequivocal evaluation of the changes introduced by the Lisbon Treaty with relation to harmonisation of penal law constitutes a quite difficult task.

The changes brought about by the Lisbon treaty allow the further unification of the system of substantive law that deals with the crimes considered to be the most challenging for the EU.

The next advantage of the Treaty of Lisbon is changing the form of legal act concerning criminal matters. Directives have been the most popular instruments in the legal heritage of the EC and applying them to criminal matters strengthens the consistency of the common legal system. However, as we have mentioned above, it is hardly possible that these directives will have any direct effect. Hence the crucial point is possibility to force the Member States to implement the directive.

The interaction between and exchange of information between the national police of the organization on Schengen territory is much more than the scope of the subordination from the international organization for police cooperation, the co-ordination of the point-by-point contact in the framework of a nationally competent structure on the line for international police cooperation. The have is a decisive sign for the posthumous goals on counteraction to the internationality of the world.

With the development of the international police cooperation that will introduce the new stuff for the interaction, it will provide additional opportunities at the national level to the competent authority for the purpose of public administration and regional security, the guardianship of the societies of the eds in the border zones and the counteraction to the accidents with the international element.

In the current security context, the cooperation with third countries and international organisations is of crucial importance for the EU's objectives of preventing and combating crime. The issue will also be an important point of discussion during the Brexit negotiations, as once the

United Kingdom will have withdrawn from the EU, new modalities of cooperation between British authorities and EU agencies will have to be identified. The current modalities of cooperation between Europol, Eurojust and their external partners, which have been analysed in this paper, may serve as a source of inspiration for the EU and UK negotiators. They also reveal the potential limits that may be faced in developing the future modalities of cooperation between the EU and the UK, and the need to reflect on developing specific modalities eventually drawing on the UK's status of former Member State. These issues are of crucial importance, since insufficient cooperation in criminal matters between the EU and the UK may reduce the safety of the people of the UK and of EU citizens.

The two agencies face challenges, starting with the need to accommodate diversity within and outside the European Union. However, their main challenge probably lies in the sensitivity of the exchange of data with third countries that are not bound by the EU norms on the protection of fundamental rights and data protection, and thus potentially entailing severe violations of fundamental rights. The two agencies are not the only actors faced with this challenge, which promises to test the effectiveness of crime prevention against legal considerations, prohibiting the processing of information when it has been obtained in violation of fundamental rights. In today's security reality, marked by regular terrorist attacks, some advocate for looser human rights standards, considering for instance that information preventing an attack shall be used, even though it may have been obtained through torture. In a European Union founded on the respect of the rule of law, such arguments are difficult to uphold. One can welcome in this regard the references in Europol's and Eurojust's regulations to the respect for data protection as a pre-requisite for the reception of personal data from third countries and the transfer of personal data to third countries. In addition, the mechanisms set up to hold both agencies accountable before democratically elected bodies and before judges shall be essential in this regard, in order to ensure that no red lines are crossed. As the Europol Regulation entered into force just a few months ago, and the Eurojust regulation is still under negotiations, it is still too early to provide a definitive answer on whether they are effective and sufficient, and a close attention will need to be paid to their practical implementation.

Security should be a key priority in a wide range of funding instruments, research and innovation programmes as well as training initiatives. Existing priorities should be adjusted as required.

The European Agenda on Security sets out the actions necessary to deliver a high level of internal security in the EU. It must be a shared agenda. Its successful implementation depends on the political commitment of all actors concerned to do more and to work better together. This includes EU institutions, Member States and EU agencies. It requires a global perspective with security as one of our main external priorities. The EU must be able to react to unexpected events, seize new opportunities and anticipate and adapt to future trends and security risks.

REFERENCES

Bigo, D. (1996). Polices en réseaux : l'expérience européenne. Paris: Presses de la Fondation nationale des sciences politiques.

Borrás, S., Koutalakis, C. and Wendler, F. (2007). European Agencies and Input Legitimacy: EFSA, EMeA and EPO in the Post-Delegation Phase. Journal of European Integration, 29(5), pp. 583–600.

Bunyan, T. (1993). Trevi, Europol and the European state. In T. Bunyan (Ed.), Statewatching the New Europe: A Handbook on the European State. London: Statewatch.

Busuioc, M. (2009). Accountability, Control and Independence: The Case of European Agencies. European Law Journal, 15(5), pp. 599–615.

Busuioc, M. (2011). European Agencies and Their Boards: Too Much Board, Too Little Monitoring. Social Science Research Network, Rochester, NY (SSRN Scholarly Paper No. ID 1890671).

Busuioc, M., Curtin, D. and Groenleer, M. (2011). Agency growth between autonomy and accountability: the European Police Office as a "living institution". Journal of European Public Policy, 18(6), pp. 848–867.

Busuioc, M. and Groenleer, M. (2012). Wielders of supranational power: the administrative behavior of the heads of European Union agencies. In M. Busuioc, M. Groenleer and J. Trondal, (Eds.), The Agency Phenomenon in the European Union: Emergence, Institutionalisation and Everyday Decision-Making. Manchester University Press: European Policy Research Unit Series, pp. 128-150.

Busuionni, M. (2010). The Accountability of European Agencies – Legal Provisions and Ongoing Practices, p. 39.

Carrapiço, H. and Trauner, F. (2013). Europol and its Influence on EU Policy-making on Organized Crime: Analyzing Governance Dynamics and Opportunities. Perspectives on European Politics and Society, 14(3), pp. 357–371.

Communication from the Commission to the European Parliament and the Council (2001). European governance: a White Paper. COM (2001) 428 final. 12.10. Brussels.

Communication from the Commission to the European Parliament and the Council (2006). Proposal for a Council Decision establishing the European Police Office. COM (2006) 817 final, 20.12. Brussels.

Communication from the Commission to the European Parliament and the Council (2002a). The operating framework for the European Regulatory Agencies. COM (2002a) 718 final, 11.12.2001. Brussels. Communication from the

Commission to the European Parliament and the Council (2002b) Democratic Control over Europol", COM (2002b) 95 final, 26.02. Brussels. Volume 13, Issue 2 (2017) Agathe Piquet 1205 Convention (1995). Convention based on article K.3 of the treaty on European Union on the establishment of a European Police Office (Europol Convention), OJ C 316/1 27.11. Brussels. Council (2003). Act of 27 November 2003 drawing up, on the basis of Article 43(1) of the Convention on the Establishment of a European Police Office (Europol Convention), a Protocol amending that Convention, OJ C 2/1 06.01.2004. Brussels. Council (2013).

Conclusions on setting the EU's priorities for the fight against serious and organised crime between 2014 and 2017. JUSTICE and HOME AFFAIRS Council meeting Luxembourg, 6 and 7 June 2013, document 12095/13. Brussels. Council (2012). Joint Statement and Common approach of the European Parliament, Council and the European Commission on Decentralised agencies, 19 July. Available on . [Accessed 15 December 2016]. Council (2009). Decision 2009/371/JAI of 4 July 2009, establishing the European Police Office, OJ L 121, 15.05. Brussels. Dehousse, R. (2008).

Curtin, D. (2017). "Brexit and the EU Area of Freedom, Security and Justice, Bespoke Bits and Pieces" in F. Fabbrini, The Law and Politics of Brexit, OUP, pp. 199.

Delegation of powers in the European Union: the need for a multi-principals model. West European Politics, 31(4), pp. 789–805.

De Bruycker, A. and A. Weyembergh. (2009). "The external dimension of the European Area of Freedom, Security and Freedom", in M. Telo, The European Union and Global Governance, (Routledge, 2009), p. 210.

De Moor, A. and Gert Vermeulen. (2010). "The Europol Council Decision: Transforming Europol into an agency of the European Union", Common Market Law Review, Vol. 47, 2010, p. 1089.

Den Boer, M. (2015). Police cooperation, a reluctant dance with the supranational EU institutions. In F. Trauner and A. Ripoll Servent (Eds.), Policy Change in the Area of Freedom, Security and Justice: How EU Institutions Matter. Routledge Studies on Government and the European Union. Abingdon: Routledge, pp. 114-132.

Egeberg, M., Martens, M. and Trondal, J. (2012). Building executive power at the European level: on the role of European Union agencies. In M. Busuioc, M. Groenleer and J. Trondal (Eds.), The Agency Phenomenon in the European Union: Emergence, Institutionalisation and Everyday Decision-Making. Manchester University Press: European Policy Research Unit Series, pp. 19-41.

Ekelund, H. (2014). The Establishment of FRONTEX: A New Institutionalist Approach. Journal of European Integration, 36(2), pp. 99-116.

EU (2016). Regulation (EU) 2016/794 of the European Parliament and of the Council of 11 May 2016 on the European Union Agency for Law Enforcement Cooperation (Europol) and replacing and repealing Council Decisions 2009/371/JHA, 2009/934/JHA, 2009/935/JHA, 2009/936/JHA and 2009/968/JHA. Brussels.

Geradin, D., Muñoz, R. and Petit, N. (Eds.) (2005). Regulation through agencies in the EU: a new paradigm of European governance. Cheltenham: Edward Elgar.

Groenleer, M., Busuioc, M. and Curtin, D. (2010). Living Europol: Between Autonomy and Accountability", Paper presented to the ECPR Fifth Pan-European Conference on EU Politics. Porto, Portugal.

Howarth, D. and Roos, M. (2017), "Pushing the Boundaries. New

Research on the Activism of EU Supranational Institutions", Journal of Contemporary European Research, this issue.

Heimans, D. (2008). "The external relations of Europol – Political, legal and operational considerations", in Bernd Martenczuck and Servaas van Thiel (eds), Justice, Liberty and Security, New challenges for EU external relations, VUB Press, p. 369.

House of Lords, EU Committee. (2008). Europol: coordinating the fight against serious and organised crime, Nov. 2008, p. 78-115.

Jorry, H. (2011). Une agence originale de l'Union : l'Agence FRONTEX. In J. Molinier (Ed.), Les Agences de l'Union Européenne. Droit de l'Union Européenne, Colloques. Bruylant, Bruxelles, pp. 169-191.

Kassim, H. and Menon, A. (2003). The principal-agent approach and the study of the European Union: promise unfulfilled?. Journal of European Public Policy, 10(1), pp. 121–139.

Kaunert, C. (2010). European internal security: towards supranational governance in the area of freedom, security and justice. Manchester: Manchester University Press. Keleman, R. D. (2002). The Politics of "Eurocratic" Structure and the New European Agencies. West European Politics, 25(4), pp. 93–118.

Kingdon, J.W. (1990). Agendas, alternatives, and public policies. New York: Harper Collins. Krapohl, S. (2004). Credible Commitment in Non-Independent Regulatory Agencies: A Comparative Analysis of the European Agencies for Pharmaceuticals and Foodstuffs. European Law Journal, 10(5), pp. 518–538.

Mihov S. (2010). Transgranichno presledvane v Shengenskoto prostranstvo, sp. Professional, br. 5, S.

Mitsilegas, V. (2017). EU Criminal Law after Brexit, Criminal Law Forum (2017) 28, p. 222.

Monar, J. (2012). The external dimension of the EU's Area of Freedom, Security and Justice, Progress, potential and limitations after the Treaty of Lisbon, Swedish Institute for European Policy Studies, p. 59.

Monar, J. (2015). The EU as an International Counter-terrorism

Actor: Progress and Constraints, Intelligence and National Security (2015) 30:2-3, p. 346.

Monar, J. (2004). "The EU as an International Actor in the Domain of Justice and Home Affairs", European Foreign Affairs Review, Vol. 4, Issue 3, p. 414.

Nikolov, P. (2015). Teoretichni i prilozhni aspekti na vzaimodeystvieto mezhdu politseyskite organi na sasedni darzhavi pri transgranichno presledvane, V: Byuletin na AMVR, Fakultet „Politsiya", br. 33, S.

Peers, S. (2015). Trends in differentiation of EU Law and lessons for the future, In Depth Analysis for the AFCO Committee of the European Parliament, 22 p.

Peers, S. (2004). Mutual Recognition and Criminal Law in the European Union: Has the Council Got it Wrong?, CMLR 41, 1, 2004, p. 5.

Roberston, S. (1997). Intelligence-Led Policing: a European Union View, in IALEIA, Intelligence Led Policing, International perspectives on policing in the 21st century, p. 12.

Trauner, F. and Auke Willems, (2016). 'The internal-external nexus: Cross-border criminal justice', Brief Issue n° 29, European Union Institute for Security Studies (EUISS), October 2016.

Van den Wyngaert, C. (2004). Eurojust and the European Public Prosecutor, In: European Area of Freedom, Security and Justice. Oxford: Oxford University Press, p. 215.

Vitorino, A. (2003). JNA Commissioner, Improving Cross-Border Cooperation between Investigating and Prosecuting Authorities. Speech 03\219, The Hague, 29.04.2003.

Vlastnik, J. (2008). Eurojust – A Cornerstone of the Federal Criminal Justice System in the EU?, In: Security versus Justise Police and Judical Cooperation in the European Union. Farnham, Surrey and London: Ashgate Publishing Limited.

Wechsler, H. (1952). 'The challenges of a Model Penal Code' Harvard Law Review 65 (1952) p. 1098.

Yanev, R., S. Mihov, P. Nikolov. (2010). Politseysko

satrudnichestvo v Shengen, V: Byuletin na AMVR, Fakultet „Politsiya", br 27, S.

Yanev, R. (2013). Politseyskoto satrudnichestvo v shengenskoto prostranstvo - chast ot vissheto spetsialno obrazovanie v Akademiyata na MVR na Republika Balgariya., Byuletin „Politsiya", br. 31, S., AMVR.

www.ingramcontent.com/pod-product-compliance
Lightning Source LLC
Chambersburg PA
CBHW071157130726
47998CB00002B/530